Emotional Dimensions of Astrology

Finding the Feeling Realms in the Horoscope

Barbara Ybarra

Copyright 2018 by Barbara Ybarra

No part of this book may be reproduced or transcribed in any form or by any means, electronic or mechanical, including photocopying or recording or by any information storage and retrieval system without written permission from the author and publisher, except in the case of brief quotations embodied in critical reviews and articles. Requests and inquiries may be mailed to: American Federation of Astrologers, Inc., 6535 S. Rural Road, Tempe, AZ 85283.

ISBN-13: 978-0-86690-670-8

Cover Design: Jack Cipolla

Published by:
American Federation of Astrologers, Inc.
6535 S. Rural Road
Tempe, AZ 85283

www.astrologers.com

Contents

Introduction	v
Chapter 1, Building a New Perspective	1
History of the study of emotions; astrology's tendency to be negative; our feeling realms; our emotional dimensions	
Chapter 2, The Lunar Node Pictures with Planets	11
Male and female energy; lunar node and mother; list of fourth harmonic aspects with lunar nodes; 24 examples	
Chapter 3, Making Word Pictures	65
The mechanics; tension between planets; definitions of houses as feelings; tension between houses; how to form word pictures	
Chapter 4, Emotional Dimensions and Emotional Memory	73
How and why we store memory; total memory; emotional transformation; two horoscopes	
Chapter 5, Three Moon Feeling Realms	83
Three adrenalin Moons, three horoscopes	
Chapter 6, Two Sun Feeling Realms	99
Feeling realms of Sun with Uranus; two horoscopes	
Chapter 7, Three Men and an Earthquake	107
Differing astro twins with Sun square Pluto; three horoscopes	
Chapter 8, The Idealism Feeling Realm	123
Two men with an idealism feeling realm; two horoscopes	

Chapter 9, Feeling Realms vs Self-sufficiency 133
    Why grand trines can be an escape; three horoscopes

Chapter 10, Matching Feeling Realms 147
    Three couples with feeling realms in the same fourth harmonic areas

Chapter 11, Emotional Places 163
    Four places that hold emotional memory; four horoscopes for events; places that are personal

Bibliography 181
Chart Data and Sources 183

Introduction

When I first started studying western astrology I wandered around, fascinated by one thing and then another, without any plan of attack. Books would come to me through my used book store angel, or from a suggestion or reference in one of the books. I barely noticed that there were different kinds of astrology, and, indeed, in the 1970s, there were fewer methods of approaching astrology. The main difference was traditional astrology versus modern astrology, either using all of the planets, or just seven of them.

Gradually I gravitated toward the psychological and the esoteric, but it turned out that I loved horary, and when John Frawley's books came out, I purchased both of them, and I loved them both, though my fascination with the practice of horary never turned into any consistent use of it. I love the psychology too much for that. I've read almost everything that Liz Greene ever wrote, and then I got tired of so much mythology. I think archetypes are helpful, but the astrology that branched out in the work of Carolyn Myss and others is sometimes difficult for people to apply to their lives.

From Noel Tyl I learned a process of deciphering psychological developmental in the horoscope. He has perfected a system of synthesis of the horoscope, using both traditional and modern techniques, and he has worked hard all his life to help people view their lives more proactively, and to understand how we are influenced from our early home. Yes, we could access memories of prior lifetimes through regression sessions, but we need only go back to the beginnings of this lifetime to see the patterns of behavior that reinforce our behavior every day.

Today there are so many processes in astrology, and many names for them, such as Evolutionary Astrology, Shamanic Astrology, and Reincarnation Astrology. The last one says that we are all living three incarnations simultaneously. Well, no wonder we need therapy! We seem to be reaching for ever more diversely spiritual ways of deciphering ourselves while we leave behind some very basic human understandings of ourselves.

Whatever our spiritual inclination or theology, each of us looks for principles that guide us through life, even when they are very practical ones. We could say we just need to "feel" what guides us. When we experience deep emotions, and when we are aware of them, afterwards we have some beliefs about where the emotions came from or why we were feeling them; and if that is so, when someone asks "What do you think?", we will have something to say. We need to have something to say, and it is vital that another person hears it.

The reason this book concentrates on emotions is because we have in our culture today thoroughly undermined the significance of them. People recognize their own talents in life before they recognize their perpetual emotions. Perpetual emotions are the ones that always come back to us again and again. If we are told as a child that we are always angry, or always sulking, or always too picky or always too sensitive, then maybe that is what we actually are always doing, never mind that someone is driving us to it. We feel inferior, embarrassed, despicable, or angry as a result, and all because we have normal human weaknesses like everyone else.

There is nothing worse than having an astrologer tell you, after looking at your chart and spotting a Sun-Saturn square, that you will always be depressed. That is not creative thinking. Our lives are given to us for soul growth. There is no horoscope we can look at that will elicit the response, "Whoopee! You must be doing everything right because this is one awesome arrangement of planets!" No, because it's actually better than that. Every horoscope is uniquely responsive to life.

This book encourages astrology students to think about the importance of feelings in life, and to consider what emotions do for us. We all want happy emotions. When the happy ones arrive it feels almost the same to everyone—wonderful! It is unhappy emotions that come in varieties and make us unique. My grandmother used to say: "When you laugh, the whole world laughs with you, but when you cry, you cry alone." I disliked it when she told me that because I thought she meant she wasn't sympathizing with me; but my grandmother was made of sympathy, so she was telling me something else. She was telling me this: "What takes away your happiness is something specific to you." Allowing of course for war and disasters, but maybe even then it is specific to you.

When people come for an astrological reading, sometimes they ask what their life purpose is. An astrologer could look at the midpoint between the Midheaven and the Ascendant and read the Sabian symbol for that degree and then talk about purpose. It's a neat trick. Sometimes people ask what their unique talent is, and the astrologer can look to see if there is a quintile aspect between planets. It's another neat trick. Ultimately, people will ask about love or money. They want happiness, but the only way to happiness is through soul growth, and the only way to soul growth is through emotional transformation.

Everyone knows that happiness is not linked to material wealth. It does seem to be true that those who find a way to appear more cheerful will then experience more wealth in their life. It is a natural law. Commerce works better when people are pleasant. In Hinduism culture there is a caste system that suggests that if you are an unworthy soul, you will be born into the lowest class and be required to stay there. This was a socio-political design to keep the lower classes from rising up out of the mud. We all know that not everyone who has money is happy, and certainly they are not all kind or wise. And yet we all strive to have more money.

Love, like money, comes with unrealistic expectations—unless you are a very spiritual person. We will never find a person who loves us unconditionally. Only God loves us unconditionally (". . . and He could be jivin'too!"). Everyone else can only give as much love as we can give back to them, and maybe they won't even give that much. In a more positive view, when one person offers forgiveness or joy to another person, and then that person returns the gift, and it continues back and forth like that, then each soul will grow in maturity, and the two souls will become one. That is the definition of a soul mate.

The best gift we can give ourselves in life is to seek our highest spiritual expression, which begins with studying our own emotions to see if we are still carrying feelings around from our past that continue to harm us, whether it be from our childhood or from another life. These types of emotions are our deepest and richest potential assets. If we are holding damaged parts of ourselves locked away, then we are hiding our best possible treasures from ourselves and others. Our relationships will suffer, and our enjoyment of any material wealth will be meager.

As you read this book, please take time to absorb the stories of the celebrities given here, to look at their horoscopes and study the aspects. I have not included personal cases because I noticed a long time ago that it is extremely easy to identify the person, and most people really don't want the public to know their best kept secrets. Celebrities pay for their fame with exposure. They have no privacy.

Following along with the astrological solar arc measurements can be tedious so I have tried not to enter an overwhelming amount of them, and I mostly use only the fourth harmonics because I am trying to prove a point here about the hard aspects. I don't use asteroids, except the occasional mention of Chiron.

As you read, try to feel what that person might have been feeling. Then look at your own chart for a time when things were changing in your life, and think about how you felt at that time. This is how we learn. In general, women are more accustomed to looking at their feelings than are men, but that does not mean they do more emotional work. It only means that they can converse more about it. In this book there are more examples of men than women, and maybe that is because there are more famous people who are men, but I don't think so. The examples here presented themselves to me and I hope they are ones you will enjoy and learn from.

A Word About Solar Arc Measurements

At this writing, it seems there are few astrologers who use solar arc measurements in chart analysis or prediction. Certainly the students of Noel Tyl use them. Vedic astrologers use a completely different system of analysis, and the Hellenistic astrologers use many other measurements. It seems that a lot of astrologers use only the planetary transits for the timing of life events, and the occasional eclipse or lunation trigger, or planetary return charts, or a host of other unique preferences; but few use solar arcs.

In my opinion, those who don't use solar arcs are missing out. Solar arcs are the easiest measurement of all to use and to depend on for meaningful insight into a person's life, not just for predictions. Solar arcs move one degree forward per year, every planet in unison, and a little slower if you are born in the summer. This means that you can use simple arithmetic. Thus, for instance, if Uranus is at 5 Aquarius, and the Sun is at 15 Aquarius at birth, we know that at age 10, or thereabout, there was a significant event or circumstance in the life of that person, because Uranus by solar arc arrived to conjunct the Sun.

The principle behind the movement of planets in that way, since it is symbolic and not literal, is that it represents how life is measured by the movement of the Sun. The Sun is our measuring stick, and you could even say that it is a divine and holy measurement. One day = one degree = one year.

The movement of the planets by solar arc is never retrograde, and it is predictably slow, taking the whole year. Because of its slow movement, if we want to be exact, we need to use an astrological computer program, or an ephemeris and long-division by 12 to decipher the speed of the Sun at the time of birth. Otherwise it might be enough to just ask someone about a particular year. The impact of a solar arc can last up to a year, but mostly it will be felt anywhere from three months prior to exact to three months afterward.

My recommendation for purposes of zooming in on important times in anyone's life is to concentrate on the fourth harmonic aspects (conjunction, square, opposition) made by solar arcs and to not look for trines or other aspects. You might notice a solar arc of a planet trine another planet at the same time as a fourth harmonic one is made; I consider this a "helper" arc. The conjunctions made by solar arc are the easiest ones to spot, but with practice it is not so difficult to notice the squares and oppositions, even without a computer program. Start with what looks significant.

In this book, I emphasize the significance of the fourth harmonic aspects, which represent the emotional themes in life. However, if you want to know when a career change is coming up, look for a solar arc that involves the tenth house ruler or is directly in aspect to the Midheaven. If you want to know if a romance is likely, look for a solar arc to the ruler of the fifth house, or the ruler of the seventh house. These areas might or might not be involved in what is here called the "feeling realms." There are of course the usual feelings that accompany career and romance changes, but they might not involve the core emotional themes in life. If you do not know your birth time, and there are many examples of that here, there will still be much that can be inferred from the meaning of the planets that are in fourth harmonic aspect to each other. In fact, they are an important key to rectifying an unknown birth time.

Solar arc movements that make fourth harmonic aspects to the natal planets that are already in fourth harmonic aspects in the chart are what I consider the "big bells" in life (borrowed phrase coined by Noel Tyl). These big bells don't go unnoticed. If they are ignored, you will have a mess on your hands, or egg on your face, because it is a seriously missed opportunity to take stock of your life. The solar arcs come around so you can engage in emotional awareness, and work on your emotional "gestalt." It is your time to "go for goal."

Solar arcs will also verify for us the importance of planets that are in very wide orb of a fourth harmonic aspect. If you have one and think it is not meaningful, check the year when the aspect became exact by solar arc. See that at age eight or nine or 10, there was the experience of an emotional event that corroborated the significance of that aspect. Anything we experience that is that powerful at a young age is going to be part of our emotional gestalt.

This happened to me at age eight when my solar arc Mars was exactly square my Saturn. There were three other solar arcs in my chart at the time, all making fourth harmonic measurements. As an adult, even after years of studying astrology, I failed to notice these; but one day, I noticed a tombstone next to my father's grave, with a girl's name on it. Apparently my mother had given birth to a stillborn baby when I turned eight, with a birthday close to mine. I had no memory of it, although I clearly remembered my brother's birth one year earlier when I was seven. The trauma must have been great. Even though I have no recall, I can see the meaning for me in the solar arcs that occurred and recognize the feelings.

Find your big bell solar arcs before you look for any transits. The big bell comes first, and the smaller bells chime in. After transits, look for any aspect from the progressed Moon, which is a small bell that can hold a powerful message. Forget the other progressions for now. When you see solar arcs, transits, and a progressed Moon all coming to the same party, you have something important to focus on.

Don't confuse yourself about which planet is doing what during a solar arc event. The planet that is moving, the one making the solar arc, is the activator. It is the one that is doing something to the natal point. However, if it is itty bitty Mercury, don't think of it as insignificant. Mercury took that long to get there, and it has something to say. Why would you consider your thinking function to be unimportant?

Here is a simple example of someone who recently experienced solar arcs that have not much to do with the emotional centers in his chart. U.S. President Donald Trump had a solar arc of Sun conjunction Ascendant when he was a candidate in May 2016. His birth time is rated AA, so we know and recognize the results of this solar arc: his sudden popularity. Whenever the Sun makes a solar arc, we hardly need to even think about what it could mean. It is a bright and shining light, bringing tremendous energy (Trump loves that word "tremendous"!) to the point of contact, which in this incidence, was the personage of Trump himself, his Ascendant. We can hardly avoid him as the media repeats his name every few minutes.

Two months later that solar arc to Trump's Ascendant had reached its peak, at the exact conjunction, and its power waned; but its job was done. By the time of the November election, another solar arc was almost exact: Pluto conjunction natal Jupiter. Any time we see those two planets working together, we know that the maximum possible effort is being made. It is about power and social expansion. Finally, we check transits and lunar progressions around the time of the election, looking for any resounding bells. There were a couple of bells on election day with transits for Trump, and on January 20, 2017, the day of inauguration, Trump's progressed Moon was exactly conjunction Venus, the ruler of his Midheaven!

The point that might be taken here is that a solar arc is not just an opportunity, for when that opportunity is taken, that energy is forever after incorporated within one's personhood. Even if not much has been accomplished within the time frame provided by the arc and then the transits, etc., there will always be an opportunity later to use what was learned at the time. This is true on all levels, both materially and spiritually, through whatever means have been taken at the time.

I included many solar arc measurements in this book to show the times in our life when our emotional dimensions are triggered into action. Since not all solar arcs are directly involved with our emotional dimensions, I have chosen only those times that are involved and avoided those that do not address these things. However, everything in life is related. Our passions motivate us into action, and then we use our actions to gauge the actions of others and make sense of life.

Chapter 1

Building a New Perspective

On April 23 and 24, 2014, Uranus, Jupiter, Mars, and Pluto were all at 13 degrees of cardinal signs from the Earth's perspective. This view is called "geocentric" because it is earth-centered, and not a scientific view, except in a subjective way. It places Earth as the center of God's creation, which is why the Catholic Church had its argument with Galileo—because we of course are the center of God's universe! Even as the scientific view becomes grander and grander, the astrological view remains a valid tool for humans because it is based on the human perspective. On April 24, 2014, the terrorist group Boko Haram went into a village in Nigeria and kidnapped hundreds of girls, enslaving them.

There are only three possible sign-sets of grand cross: the cardinal, the fixed, and the mutable. If you have a conjunction, square, or opposition in your chart, the planets are near each other in degree in one of these three "modalities" (not counting when we include a planet that has wandered into the next modality but is still close in degree).

This book's purpose is to help build a new perspective on the nature of the fourth harmonic aspect. Though some humanistic astrologers have been saying for years that these aspects are neither good or bad, the language that we are accustomed to says otherwise; often it is conveyed to the owner of the chart that the task to "overcome" these aspects requires a disconnected approach, not an integration of what is there, but a defiance against our fate. We need to develop a more comprehensive view of dealing with ourselves.

Feeling Realms and Emotional Dimensions

Deep down, all of us are intimately connected with the planets because we all carry those same mythological stories within us. The planets are the outer and mythological manifestations of the inner needs that propel us into action on Earth. When an astrologer is looking at a horoscope, he or she is looking at a picture of a soul in action, even though the horoscope is a snapshot of the solar system at just one moment in time. That moment includes all the suggestions we need to show us where in our lives our greatest development can occur.

Humans are sentient beings: we feel and then we act; we act and then we feel. We also have a great amount of free will and the potential for self-awareness, so we spend a lot of time thinking and reflecting, which serves to heighten and deepen our emotions. If not for our emotions, humans might analyze all over the place, and make logical choices that benefit the welfare of all, much like ants cooperating for the preservation of the colony. We might just sit around talking most of the time, accomplishing very little, having agreed to limit the propagation of our species, and thus limit our requirements for action. It's a very odd thing to consider. Without emotion there would be no art or music, and no reason to smile or cry.

I think most of us would agree that our feelings have great power over our actions, and that even after much thinking and planning, it is still our feelings that give us direction in life. We so often hear people say "follow your heart"! As an astrologer, I have come to care more and more about where in the horoscope we see our emotional centers, and how people can benefit from the awareness of them.

It's no surprise to astrologers that our chronically troublesome emotions in life are linked to square, opposition, or conjunction aspects in the natal chart. The tension of them will vary in strength, depending on which planets and signs are involved, but in general these configurations are always accompanied by serious challenges. There is no refuting that. Unfortunately, astrology has been persistently pessimistic about these hard aspects, adopting a doomsday approach to them. Conversely, the view of a trine in the chart (the blessed 120°!), which is symbolically tensionless, has long been considered to be everything fortunate (again, not so true).

We need to improve the language and the perspective surrounding these aspects (the 0°, 90°, and 180° separations) so that we can learn to honor and appreciate these as engines for soul growth. The placement of the planets, if astrology is to be believed at all, is a custom fit for us, located within the framework of time, for our benefit—and certainly not for our punishment. The hard aspects need to be given the highest honor, not the lowest. They are there for our transformation so that we can move from old frustration toward co-creation with the divine.

My decision to call this book *The Emotional Dimensions of Astrology* came about because I was given that title by astrologer Noel Tyl before he knew that I would write a book and before I knew what it would be about. He never told me what he thought I should write about; he only gave me the title—as a gift. As I mulled over in my mind where that title would take me, I began to think of the importance of emotion, and how little credence we give to it.

What immediately comes to mind with emotion in astrology is the natural tendency for us to see the water signs as an expression of emotion and the perception of the Moon as emotional fulfillment. Neither of these is what I think of as an indicator of one's emotional center. A simpler view of the Moon can assign to it the function of nurturing. Just as the Sun is all about standing up for our individuality, the Moon is about sitting down (so to speak) and taking care of ourselves. The Moon function might be perfectly unimpeded, and therefore not be a dynamic emotional center at all. Even though there are ordinary feelings that accompany nurturance, such as pleasure, urgency, relief, etc., unless the Moon is in a hard aspect with another planet, it will normally accomplish what it needs to accomplish without much ado.

The concept of the "feeling realms" is something I developed while thinking about our emotional centers—our deep interaction with the world. I started seeing the planets in the hard aspects as places for emotional growth, a bit like countries which form alliances with other countries for possible gain, while accepting the risk that comes with the rewards. The word "feeling" was chosen because "emotional" realms sounded much too turbulent to me, even though the feeling realms are indeed places to hold our most turbulent emotions. These places must be considered as sacred to us, so that we do not despise or ignore them.

Unfortunately, our language has not developed enough to suit these kinds of discussions. The word "emotion," etymologically, means "acting out what we feel"; but common usage of it has made it interchangeable with the word "feelings," which is fine because we have so few words to talk about it. Also, emotional expression is a different subject from the inner experience of it, but we have no words to differentiate that either. We also do not have words that distinguish between everyday feelings of pleasure and discomfort, and the deeper, longer lasting emotions that we carry around for life. Because of all that, many of us doubt that we even have important emotions, and we consider emotion to be incidental to our circumstances rather than integral to the development of our souls.

As my ideas came together, the phrase "emotional dimensions" came to mean for me the structures that people build within their feeling realms to hold emotional memories. These, of course, are imaginary places, but the brain, the gut, and the heart may very well function like that, building tiny, miniature structures within our cells for the purposes of recording and holding these emotional memories. The figurative image looks like a building (a castle? a mansion?), certainly with at least three imaginary dimensions, and more if we include the construct of time. All of it together is what we have created and organized within us, or left disorganized. We add on rooms and artifacts as we go along, during strong transits or solar arcs to the planets within these feeling realms.

So, out of the blue, out of the title for this book, came my first need to help rework the old habit of projecting a negative view of the hard aspects in the horoscope, and then, after that, to help define what these aspects actually do for us. The language astrologers have inherited that centuries ago was so constructive and instructive now limits our development as humans. When we are told that we have a blocked set of energies in the natal chart (in ourselves), we immediately feel that we are less fortunate than others, or we feel guilty of some horrible crime. However, when we are able to locate these strong emotions within ourselves, with grace and acceptance, we can begin to do the work which we came here to do—our soul transformation.

Two Types of Feeling Realms

In my proposal there are two types of feeling realms in the horoscope. The first type is the lunar nodal axis—our foundation of trust, which is our primary feeling realm. By its very nature the Moon's nodal axis is an opposition, and it suggests the particular kind of social tension and situation in which we find ourselves. When we are newborns, our parents consider us to be blank slates, and they wonder what we will become when we grow up, but the truth is that we already resemble the social situation in which we are born. Since the nodes are the points where the Moon crosses the path of the Sun (the mom and the dad), esoterically it brings in both the male and female energy;

but it is from the mother we receive this first feeling realm, even while we are still in her womb.

The second type of feeling realm is any fourth harmonic aspects in the chart. There can of course be additional planets compounding the first feeling realm with the lunar nodes. If there are a lot of planets there with the nodes, in conjunction (or square) them, it will feel to that person as if the interaction with others within society is very full, filled with complex situations among people. This can become either a great task or a great resignation, because we always need to accept our lunar node situation as our basic trust in life (more on that later).

All fourth harmonic aspects come with tension and intense emotion. Though we live with emotion every single day, we tend to fear the power of it, and we sense that it needs to be managed somehow. We all instinctively know that living too tightly entwined with our emotions, and not knowing what to do with them, can be, at the very least, suffocating or chaotic, which is exactly why people look for ways to avoid the whole mess. Also, because some of us try so hard not to spill our excessive emotional energy all over others, we don't give other people permission to do so either, or even tell us about it. It is all because we have no consensus of understanding for it, and no structure with which to proceed.

The history of studying feelings and emotions in our Western world goes back to the early Greek times, and wonderfully, there we find the mythological stories that have everything to do with our experience of emotions. The intellectual study of emotion, which began in the middle 1800s, brought a much more clinical approach, and that is unfortunately when and where our dissociation begins. The explosion of psychology in the early 1900s landed in the clinical basket. Theory after theory was devised to describe how as humans we learn or don't learn to interact with one another, how development occurs in early childhood, and what sort of behavior is social and what sort is antisocial.

The rush to establish scientific processes for everything became a priority. We stumbled right over a deeper look at emotions, except for a certain branch of psychology. Yes, people have asked about the value of emotions, but then immediately sought the cures for unwanted emotions, which is similar to our approach in the biological world, where we treat symptoms instead of causes.

Everything in science is aimed at getting rid of pain and discomfort. Mid twentieth century psychologists favored behaviorism, the study of what makes us act in certain ways and how to get rid of the unwanted actions. Western astrology followed their lead. Astrologer Alan Leo and others, like Pavlov, talked about behavior, and our psychological tendencies. If Alan saw Mars and Pluto conjunct in the fourth house of the parent, he probably inferred that the father set the example for violent behavior, and the person would also likely be violent in some way. That's as far as it went. As a society, we refused to acknowledge the value of the emotions themselves, or what they mean to us.

The horoscope is first and foremost a picture of our feelings. The horoscope can suggest, of course, ordinary, everyday things that happen in life, especially represented by planets unimpeded (the ones not in hard aspects)—Mars for initiative, Venus for compliance, Mercury for communication, etc., and we feel the need to execute all of these functions in life. The planets that are in hard aspect, however, are more than ordinary needs; they are extraordinary needs because they are under "high developmental tension." If you search the Internet for that phrase, by the way, Noel Tyl's name will appear on the screen. It means that in the early home there were situations present that pressurized and often obstructed certain areas of our development. These situations, and the resulting emotions, complicate things, and increase the drive for the fulfillment.

Freud, who was called the father of psychology, came up with his famous "drive theory" in the early 1900s. He stated that when a need is not met, it becomes full of negative tension, which in turn increases the motivation to meet the need. When the drive is sufficient to meet the need, the tension releases and the person can relax. This theory works pretty well with rudimentary needs such as food and sex. But with extraordinary needs, such as the ones in our feeling realms, the drive never subsides because it encompasses a set of complex, dynamic feelings. It can only continue to transform. We know that Freud was an atheist, so he entertained no thoughts on soul development.

Many psychologists after Freud came closer to bringing self-development to greater awareness, but it was not a big priority. Psychologist Abraham Maslow contributed to the mainstream understanding of these concepts in America, which were presented at every school health class. He introduced his hierarchy of needs theory as a pyramid, much like the popular food pyramid. His idea was that we cannot give love if we haven't met our more basic survival needs. As we acquire one level of needs, we move onto the next level, culminating in self-actualization or spiritual advancement. Though there are some problems with this theory, it depicts humans as wanting to develop in every way possible that we can, not just materially or intellectually.

Regardless of where we think we are in that pyramid, some of the needs depicted in the horoscope are ordinary needs, and some are extraordinary needs that require extraordinary attention and can provide us with extraordinary rewards. The central emotions that we find ourselves in on any given day are our thematic ones, and they appear to be pre-birth conditions of our soul. They are "reflected" in the conditions of the home, not "caused by" the conditions in the home. The truth is that regardless of beliefs in reincarnation or in the Christian belief of "original sin," blaming our parents for how we feel is inappropriate. That doesn't mean we have to like or admire them, or to be unconcerned with our legacy, but it does mean that we need to take responsibility for our own feelings and actions at some point in our life.

It is not easy or even necessary to sort out all of life's complexities, but our central emotions in our feeling realms are what drives us forward, and they color everything we do, no matter what our level of development. These fourth harmonic areas of life can be described as being "short-circuited" because of the tension that is present (yet another turn of phrase by Noel Tyl). For instance, a young man whose father is an alcoholic may not believe that he is worthy of obtaining good employment. When he goes for an interview, even though he may already have acquired the necessary skill set, he shows little confidence during the interview. Suppose that this is reflected in his tenth house ruler being opposed to his second house ruler—an obvious example, but a good one. The person's feelings of self-worth are in tension with his feelings about making a place for himself in the world, so his needs are short-circuited. Here is a general description of the term as it is used in electronics:

> "In circuit analysis, a short circuit is a connection between two nodes that forces them to be at the same voltage. This means there is no resistance and no voltage drop across the short... With low resistance in the connection, a high current exists, causing the cell to deliver a large amount of energy in a short time." (online courses, Dr. Holbert)

Too much energy is too much energy. The reason there is too much energy for someone in certain areas is because there are emotional memories that have not yet been resolved. These emotions could be thought of as early childhood events which have continued to have an effect, or it could be thought of as past life events which have yet to be resolved. Both do the same thing—they push us to find solutions. If we are convinced that wealth and status are what we want and need, there might be inappropriate overcompensation in the rush to get it, and we can end up with something that does not make us happy. That short circuit will flummox us until we understand where it comes from.

When we are able to locate the strong feelings within ourselves that are linked to our ability to function well, or not so well, we have found our treasure trove: the emotional work that leads to our creativity. Astrologers can offer word descriptions of these feeling realms, of what we see in the birth chart, and that in turn can help people recognize themselves and begin to work with their emotional dimensions. That is of course, if they are listening, and they are ready to hear it.

Chapter 2

The Lunar Node Pictures with Planets

Before getting down to the nitty-gritty of the feeling realms showcased in this book, some groundwork must be established for the fundamental parts of ourselves that define how we operate. All humans are basically comprised of the same parts except that we have varying degrees of soul development, and a myriad of ways in which we express ourselves, which are linked to the twelve archetypes of the zodiac signs.

In all of us there is both male and female energy. As psychiatrist Carl Jung has pointed out with his anima and animus stories (the yin and yang in us), humans have diverse amounts of feminine and masculine energy within them, with both positive and negative expressions of them. It turns out that some women are just more aggressive than others, and some men are more nurturing than others; but we are nevertheless all microcosms of the whole.

The two lights, the Sun and the Moon, represent the male and female energies. They are equally indispensable, and they are also inseparable from each other. The physical male has for eons experienced life as adventurous. It was required of him. The Sun energy represents our need for individual stature—the need to stand up for the self and others, and it tends to "rhyme" with things like courage. The physical female has for eons experienced life as the nurturer, since it was required of her. It is the feeling of taking care of self and others and it "rhymes" with empathy and tenderness. What we don't balance out within ourselves between the male and female energies, we usually look for in a partner.

Other planets that are assigned to male or female energy in astrology can be ambiguous about the whole thing, such as when Venus is in Aries, or Mars is in Pisces. Saturn, which has a connection with masculinity, is nevertheless representing something other than being male. It can operate sufficiently in any sign and through either parent as it teaches us our boundaries and responsibilities. Although Saturn has traditionally been the task of the father to bestow his expectations and approval on his children, anyone can take on that parenting role.

We can ask ourselves if there is a feminine counterpart for Saturn in the chart. What planet or situation in the chart symbolizes the mother's traditional task to pass along instructions to her children? Her instruction would be different from the father's instruction, and it would be for engagement in social situations, which do not especially pertain to responsibility and boundaries; they instead require trust and immersion within the whole.

If Saturn is the task of the father figure, then the Moon's nodes are the task of the mother figure. The sharing of the nodal situation, imparted from the mother even before birth, can be called the foundation of trust in our life, our first primary understanding of our social context within this world. It is a picture of how we feel about fitting in comfortably among others. It is where we recognize our self as accepted and appreciated within the group, even without accomplishments. This is the lunar nodes, our primary feeling realm.

Moon's Nodes

Over time the use of the lunar nodal axis to view the mother figure in the early home was developed, and then extended to the experience of the person in the general social situation. It proved to be profoundly correct. Noel Tyl writes that there is in the Moon's Nodes the potential for "a knot of complication through the mother, or indeed, an amalgamation of strengths through the maternal influence" (*Synthesis and Counseling in Astrology*, 2004). This is a beautiful statement, which describes for us both the inevitable tension in the experience, along with the possibility of strong positive development over time.

The influence of the Moon's nodes from the mother quite naturally precludes all of the effects of the father influence. It operates before the father guidance gets a chance to operate. This is not to say that the gentle touch of a father holding his baby is insignificant, but as a function, nurturing is always a yin trait. This fact is backed by the work of prominent psychologist Erik Erikson, as seen in his book *Identity and Life Cycle* (1959). Erikson writes that there are stages of psychosocial development that all people experience in common. The first stage is trust (he calls it trust vs. mistrust) and it lasts from birth until about age eighteen months. Up until that age, we have little interest in or ability to defy our mothers, or even to please her or anybody else. We simply wait for someone to take care of us, and trust that everything will be okay. We very rarely are told no. Even when we finally are given rules, they do not make much sense to us, and the Saturn function of self-discipline does not truly begin to take effect until around age seven.

The Moon's nodal axis has a cycle of about eighteen and a half years, in which it travels back to its original position. Like Saturn, this first cycle signifies a kind of initiation into the world. At around age eighteen we are ready to take what we've learned from our lunar node situation and try it on for size in the real world, without our mother's recommendation or direct influence. We go to college or we get a job. We move out of the house or we at least gain more freedom from our ties with mother. Of course many mother situations are not conventional and mother can be someone who is not of the family, or even an institution.

The trust situation evolves into an ever greater social one, but it retains its original flavor. It is important to remember that it is not quite a function, unless it is the function of "gathering"; it is a condition for trust. It is where we find ourselves, almost by accident, being drawn into the social situations described in our horoscope. If our trust conditions in the lunar node picture are complicated by many planets in hard aspects, then we are more compelled to work out the tension between those functions in order to appease our trust in life. People do this in different ways. Some will become very involved in the world of other people, and some will retreat into themselves, like Edward Gorey in chapter eight.

It has been popular recently in Western astrology to divide the lunar nodes into past and present lives. Astrologer Jeffrey Green had much to do with the popularization of that notion in Western astrology, of viewing the South Node as the past life indicator and the North Node as the current one. He first wrote about his ideas in *Pluto: The Evolutionary Journey of the Soul*, vol.1 (1985). He does not mention the mother in the home, or anything specifically about social conditions and trust. His book is complex, esoteric, and meaningful for many, but it could also be irrelevant for those who are not convinced of reincarnation or cannot relate to it very well. Also, when using reincarnation as a basis for soul study, the tendency can be to romanticize a past life, or to put blame on others, or become indifferent to our responsibility in this current life, all of which can be a pitfall to soul growth.

Astrologers Noel Tyl and Jeffrey Green can be said to offer similar processes from very different approaches because both of them are offering a view of ourselves at a fundamentally core level. Though Tyl does not emphasize the importance of the mother in every single horoscope (just as he does not emphasize the importance of the father in every case), he has outlined an excellent process for it. The mother in the early home is not just *any* person. She is the very person who is able to reflect back to us our requirements for trust in social situations and what we require in life in order to interact with others.

It is sufficient, I think, to treat the Moon's nodes as an axis, and not necessarily as a framework of past and present, of what we have already done and what we need to do next. The Moon's nodes are an illusory dichotomy between our individual expression and the social situations in which we find ourselves, but not a dichotomy of self against society. Our encounters with life produce intense feelings, beginning with the first time we step away from our mother and a classmate takes advantage of us, or conversely, the first time we push another student. In these moments, the North and South Nodes are encountered simultaneously. There is no division. Our experience is a totality in time.

The lunar node situation can be described by house and sign and by aspects to the planets or the angles. To be in the conditions that resonate with our lunar nodal situation is our bottom line requirement in life. When all else seems to have gone wrong in life, we can still recognize ourselves in the underlying presence of these conditions, and for that reason, we can use the words "trust is there as long as there is . . . " and then describe the conditions.

The Moon's nodes are greatly colored by planets in fourth harmonic aspect to them. Other aspects are significant as well, but certainly not as influential as the hard aspects. When I first read the first volume of Jeff Green's Pluto book, I thought that the connection between Pluto and the nodes was a bit forced in favor of Pluto being the ultimate evolution of our soul; I wasn't convinced of it. Then I came across this quote in his book: "When planets aspect the nodal axis, and Pluto has no direct aspects with the nodes, then those planets have played a major role (by house, sign, and aspect) in shaping the kinds of experiences that the person has had for evolutionary or karmic reasons."

This made much more sense to me, but Green left it at that, and didn't go into further into the development of it. In my view, the South Node, in spite of it possibly representing a past life, does not really represent what we have "left behind." Is it possible to leave behind old wisdom? Or is it possible to dismiss old mistakes? No, because we must mend them, or we have learned from them. Our brains and our hearts are complex, and so is our elimination process (the south end of the nodal axis).

The Eastern view of the Moon's nodes, as used in Vedic astrology, seems a little different from our Western view. Literature refers to it as a "dragon," and it is considered altogether dangerous at either end. It can be ravenous at its head (North Node) and angry at its tail (South Node). The simple understanding of this is that the nodal axis can operate in a reactive way until we know what governs its needs. Neither end can be left to operate without governance; but if we are feeding the dragon the right food (the right conditions in our present life), then the assimilation process has a good start, and, poetically, our dragon becomes an Oborous through acceptance of the now, the Tao of our current life.

Below are some descriptions of the Moon's nodes in hard aspect to the planets and angles. These are examples of how we can make word descriptions based on the signs of the lunar nodes, along with the functions of the planets involved. These are simple descriptions which can be refined by the client in consultation, but the idea is to try and keep them simple so that is easy to apply them to our lives.

A Note on Orbs

Some astrologers have tried to keep aspects to the Moon's nodes within very small orbs of influence, just one or two degrees. I don't know how that evolved, but probably it was from treating the nodal axis as if it were a point of special interest. My belief is that the Moon's Nodes are every bit as important as the Sun and Moon in the chart, because it is the interaction between them that gave birth to us; therefore an orb of up to

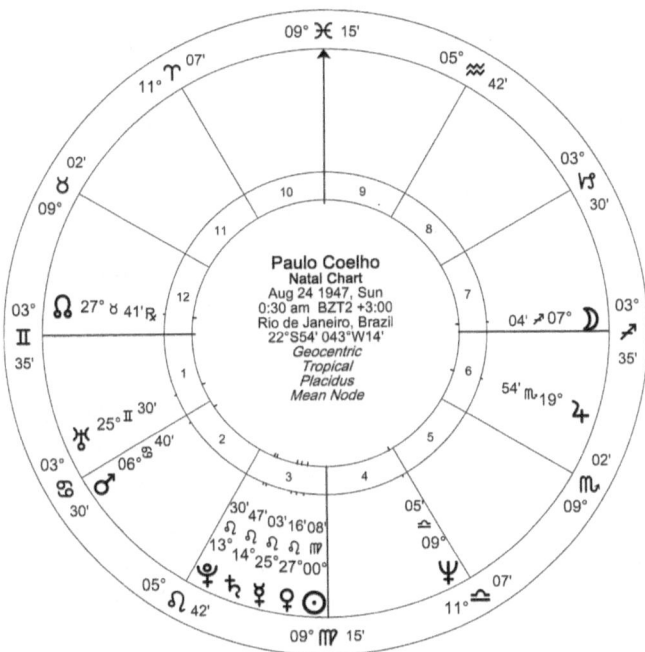

ten degrees would not be out of the question. I say this because I see it operating in the lives of people with wide orbs, though not everyone with a wide orb is able to define it as something important to them.

Lunar Nodes with Ascendant-Descendant

Paulo Coehlo

Celebrities commonly have a need to be on stage, but not everyone with this aspect naturally arrives on stage, nor does every celebrity have this aspect. Popular mystical author Paulo Coelho who wrote *The Alchemist* (1988) has the lunar nodal axis in Taurus-Scorpio very close to his Ascendant-

> **The lunar nodes in fourth harmonic aspect to the Ascendant-Descendant axis is the need to be on stage in order to trust in life.**

Emotional Dimensions of Astrology

Descendant axis. It is also square his Sun, Mercury, and Venus near the fourth house angle. The square to the Sun reemphasizes his strong need to be important, but the aspect to the Ascendant axis is specifically asking for public presentation of his body or his name.

When he was a teen, Paulo's parents sent him to a mental hospital for "extreme introversion," quite a surprising diagnosis for someone with the nodal axis on the Ascendant.[1] The accusation of introversion may have been his parent's way of preventing him from becoming a writer, since they had their heart set on him becoming a lawyer or an engineer. Today he spends much time behind a microphone at seminars and workshops. He was even on a debate team in high school, which is hardly the activity of a young person who was especially introverted.

We could say that Paulo can trust in life as long as he is visibly communicating (third house stellium) and offering his idealism to the world (the Venus-Mercury conjunction) as he creates his stories about the deep (Scorpio) and grounding (Taurus) journeys in which we find ourselves. As we go along in life, like the traveler in Paulo's *The Alchemist*, we discover that our material world is complementary to our inner world. This is a very beautiful expression of the Taurus-Scorpio dichotomy. Chart Data: A rating

Noel Tyl

Astrologer Noel Tyl has the Moon Nodal axis in Sagittarius-Gemini, six degrees from his Ascendant-Descendant axis. His early career was as an opera singer. As many people know, opera is the most flamboyant and extravagant genre for dramatic presentation of the self, probably even more so than heavy metal rock concerts. His deep and powerful voice also aids him in his dramatic lectures in astrology. The lunar nodal axis is also square (five degrees) natal Neptune, which rules his Midheaven.

---

[1] From "Boy from Ipanema" by Markia Schaertl on PC blog on Paulo Coelho, December 2007, retrieved October 2015.

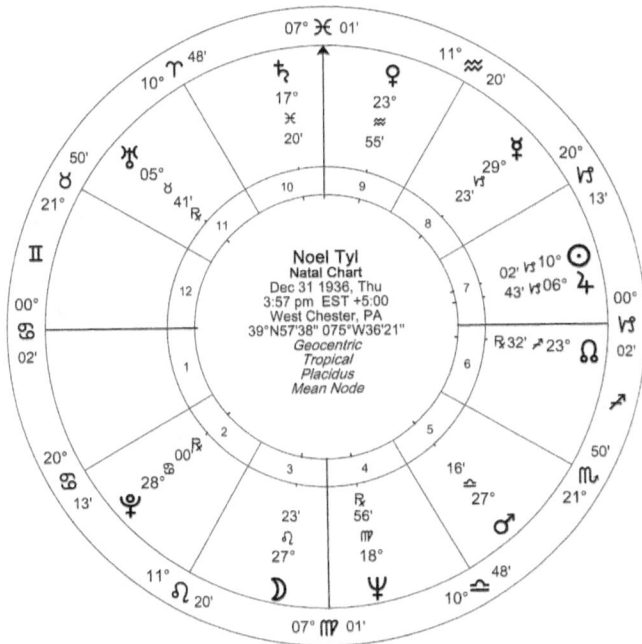

We could say that Noel can trust in life as long as he has a stage on which to present his life's work, in order to communicate (Gemini) to others and bring inspiration (Sagittarius), through either the performing arts or his more esoteric endeavors in astrology (Neptune). Chart Data: A rating

Janis Joplin

Rock-n-roll superstar Janis Joplin had her lunar nodal axis conjunction her Ascendant-Descendant in Aquarius-Leo, and also square Uranus. You cannot have a more distinctive stage presence profile than that. She did what she needed to do in her life, except of course for taking too many drugs. It is significant to note that Venus and Mercury, also in Aquarius, are in the twelfth house, suggesting that she needed to hide her true idealism with an "I don't care" attitude (more on idealism in chapter eight).

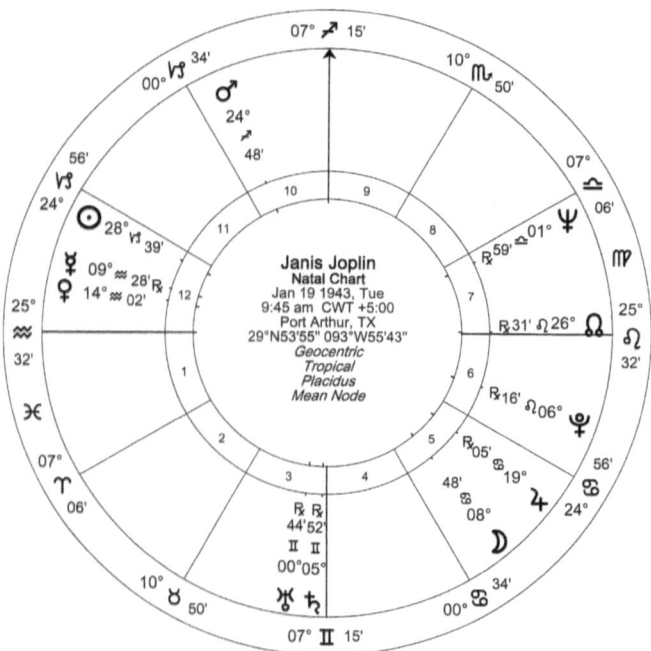

We could say that Janis could trust in life as long as she could be on stage in her avant-garde way (Aquarius), entertaining others (Leo), and bring a unique communication style that could break the mold (Uranus and Saturn in Gemini in the third house). Everyone said of Janis that her energy on stage was "electric," which had nothing to do with stage lighting

It would be instructive to have had an interview with Janis Joplin because she came from a very conservative middle class family in Texas, and she was expected by her parents to meet the family standards, to marry nicely and have a good career if she needed one. The mother may have been creative too, judging by the Moon-Neptune square, or her mother may have been a person who lived by appearances.

At one point in Janis' life early on, she adopted a tidy hairdo and went to college and worked, and then became engaged; but

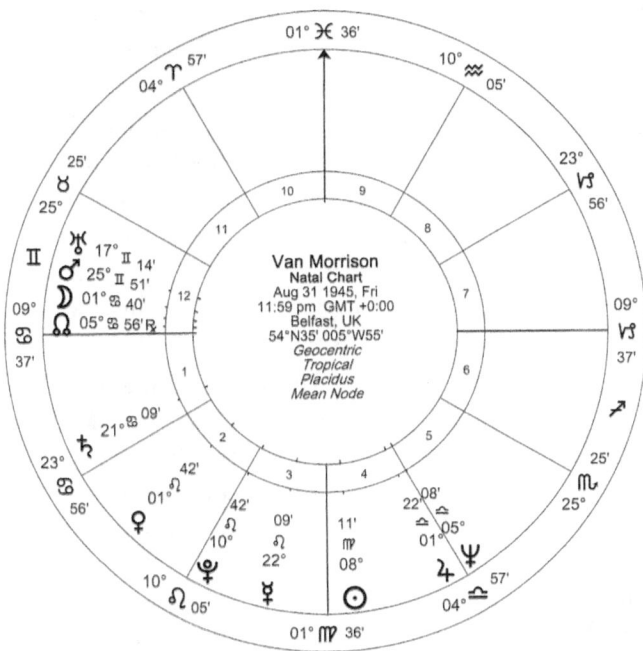

it didn't last. In many cases when a woman's lunar nodes are in contact with the Ascendant there can be too much pressure from the mother on the appearance, pushing the child to look and act a certain way—and then the whole thing explodes. It can happen with men as well, but I have noticed it in the case of women especially, because the mothers are their role models. Chart Data: A rating

Van Morrison

Irish soul singer Van Morrison has the lunar nodal axis very close to the Ascendant-Descendant axis, and also conjunction the Moon and square Neptune in the fifth house, which rules the Midheaven. This is very fitting for Van and for the Irish people in general, to be appreciated on stage for that loose and wandering singing style he has that connects people with their emotions. Morrison also has Jupiter and Chiron square the nodes, so there is an added sense of what we might call the flamboyant chronic sufferer. Anyone who is familiar with his music has heard those plaintive notes in his songs.

Morrison's Ascendant is in Cancer, suggesting resonance with the closely-knit Irish culture. Emotion comes out in Irish music, poetry, and tales, routinely in their pubs, which are places designated for emotional release. I've been to Ireland and can report that the people there are not emotional until they get into a pub; and it is not necessarily the liquor that does it. Those who drink tea there are the same way.

Van Morrison's mother was a singer herself, and his father owned a very large collection of musical albums which he played all the time. They both encouraged their son toward his musical career;

> **The Moon's nodes in fourth harmonic with the Midheaven-Nadir axis: the need to take responsibility for the group, or in the profession, in order to trust in life.**

and there doesn't seem to be any sad backstory to his life, except the things that we all have happen in our lives. Van merely was born into one of the most musically concentrated houses in Ireland, and he was immersed in the gestalt of the people, which is deeply melancholic.

We could say that Van Morrison can trust in life as long as he can bring his art to the stage, and share his understanding of connection (Cancer) between people, and express his poetic fanaticism (Jupiter with Neptune). Chart Data: A rating

So, all in all, a statement that can be made for anyone with the lunar nodal axis in fourth harmonic aspect to the Ascendant-Descendant could be:

> "You can trust in life as long as you can allow yourself to be on stage somehow, either physically or vocally present to the public, or in some smaller way physically prominent in the community as a role

model or an advocate of some sort. The need is to be recognized, and only secondarily to be appreciated and applauded."

Lunar Nodes with Midheaven-Nadir

This configuration can occur in a small way, just as the need to be on stage can occur in a small way. Many with this aspect will take on family responsibilities that other members of the family will not take. People with this configuration feel they must or will have added responsibility in their lives; or they feel that the world is asking something of them that only they can give.

Robert Kennedy

Robert Kennedy, the younger brother of John Kennedy, had his lunar nodal axis in Cancer-Capricorn conjunction the Midheaven-Nadir by eight degrees. Jupiter and the Moon are also close to the Midheaven, emphasizing the public nature of his responsibility in life, and his awareness of being publicly driven.

The Kennedy clan mother, Rose, was said to have been as influential on the children as the father had been. Both parents pressured the children to succeed in the world, to be connected, to be bigger than life, especially in politics. In his book *Robert Kennedy, Brother Protector*, James Hilty states that the mother, Rose, heavily influenced Robert as a child. According to author Judie Mills in *Robert Kennedy—His Life*, "Robert took to heart his mother's agenda" of making everything and every minute of his life count for something important.

Jupiter, so involved with the Midheaven in Capricorn, was all about feeling the responsibility to live up to the legacy of that important family name. Jupiter ruled the eighth house of inheritance, the shared story that all Kennedys were asked to accept. We could say that Robert Kennedy could trust in life as long as he could commit himself to the governing of the people (Moon in Capricorn), and live up to the shared karma of the Kennedy

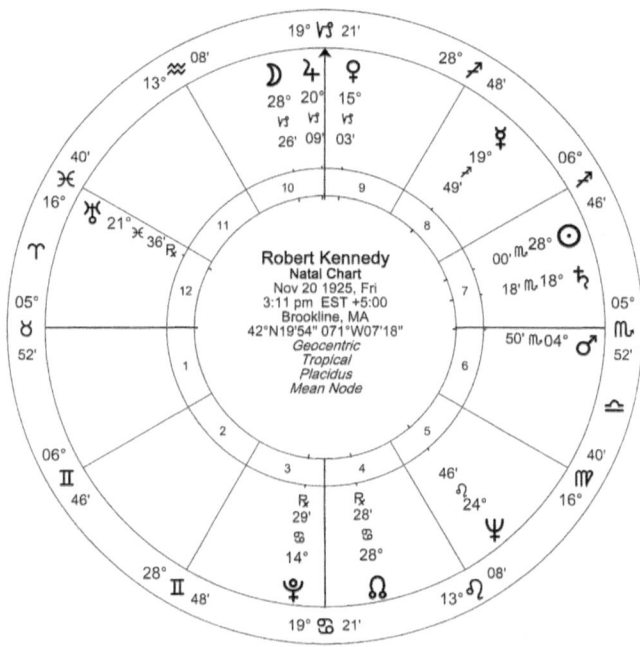

name. Probably as a younger brother, he even thought of it as fealty, as much to his country as to his mother.

There has been a lot of death in the Kennedy family, and perhaps there was prescience in the family from the beginning, that their lives would be filled with tragedy. Notice that Venus in the eighth house is disposited by Jupiter. In a simple way, we could say that Jupiter "owes" something to Venus; it owes allegiance to Venus because of its difficult task. Notice that Venus rules the third house of siblings and is square Uranus in the twelfth house. It is a story that we cannot help but see, knowing that Robert had to endure the death of his brother the way he did. It gets more complex if we think about the fact that Venus rules the Ascendant in Robert's chart, so he no doubt modeled himself after his brother from the beginning.

The responsibility that Robert felt in life was just who he was, but it held the foundation of many painful memories in his life.

This is how a chart holds together for meaning when we look at it. The parts of a horoscope are coherent when we have the ability to see it. What looks at first to be disjointed, is our lack of ability as astrologers. Chart Data: A Rating

Denzel Washington

Actor Denzel Washington has the Moon Nodal axis very close to his Midheaven-Nadir, which is also closely aligned with the Sun and Mercury in Capricorn. Denzel often wonders if he didn't do the right thing, which was to become a preacher/minister.[2]

Many of his movie roles portray people who took a stand on a moral principle or who stood up for others. Denzel played the parts of Malcolm X, Steve Bilko, an apartheid activist, a wrongly convicted boxer named Rubin Carter, and many other roles which reflect his commitment to being the responsible agent in life, or at least representing those who have taken on certain responsibilities.

Washington also has the Moon's nodes in a square to the Ascendant-Descendant axis. When this happens and there is connection to both of the angles the person will have a very public life. We could say that Denzel can trust in life as long as he can be on stage and shine for those in this world who have stood for responsibility and commitment. He once said in an interview that a woman in his mother's hair salon prophesied to him when he was a little boy that one day he would speak to many people and help mankind.

I think Denzel's mother must have been a firecracker of a person. Denzel's Moon is peregrine in Aquarius at the end of the fourth house, rushing into the fifth house of performance. His mother doted on him so he would have the confidence to go out and preach like his father; but I don't think he has ever disap-

---

[2]From an article by Xan Brooks, "I don't want movie-star firends"; interview with Denzel Washington; The *Guardian*, January 24, 2013.

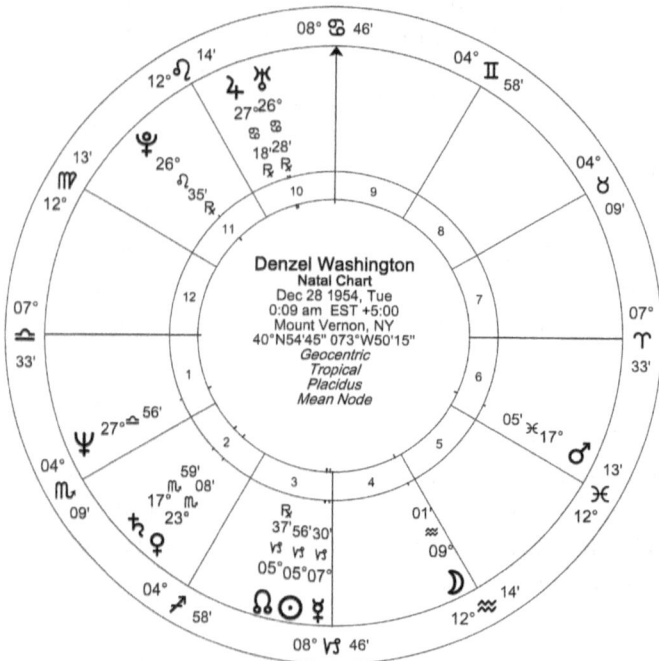

pointed her for not doing it.

Probably his most difficult feeling realm in life is the Venus-Saturn conjunction, but when we consider the religious father, we must make allowances for the insistence on building self-respect through responsibility to earn love of self and others. If Denzel loves himself and his family today, then he has done much emotional work to achieve that transformation (more on Venus-Saturn in another chapter). Chart Data: AA rating

A statement that can be made for any person who has the lunar nodes in fourth harmonic aspect with the MC-IC axis is:

> "You can trust in life as long as you find yourself in situations where you have taken on added responsibility in life, or have assumed a position of authority to lead others, either in your profession or in your own family or community."

Lunar Nodes with the Sun

With this configuration, the mother in the early home put a spotlight on the child in a way that the father could not. Probably much was expected from the child, but also a great amount of attention and appreciation was conferred, even for no particular reason. This is usually a good situation if it is not overdone and if the mother doesn't act like the Christ child is in her living room. There can be negative expressions of it as well. The mother might have been propelled by jealousy, and needed to use the child to gain attention for herself; but usually it is a positive expression.

> Lunar nodes in fourth harmonic with the Sun is the need to shine in order to trust in life.

Prince William

Many royal people have been born during an eclipse. Prince William, Duke of Cambridge, was born a few hours after a partial solar eclipse, so we will forgive him the fourteen degrees between the Sun and the Moon's nodes. Princess Diana doted on her son. It's not that the father, Prince Charles, was left out of the picture, but the mother somehow overcompensated for any lack of enthusiasm from the father.

Notice also that there is a more exact aspect with the lunar nodes square Saturn. This, too, was the need for Diana to be the parent who was both mother and father to her child. Charles perhaps was just not fully present in the marriage, and we saw much in the media of his later bonding time with his sons. Prince Harry has the natal Moon in wide opposition to Saturn, confirming that the mother also took on father duty early in his life.

The Sun was exact by solar arc conjunction to the lunar nodes in William's chart one year prior to Diana's death by car accident; this was at the time that Diana and Charles were divorced. William's understanding of his relationship with his mother came into sharp focus for him that year (1996) when the divorce

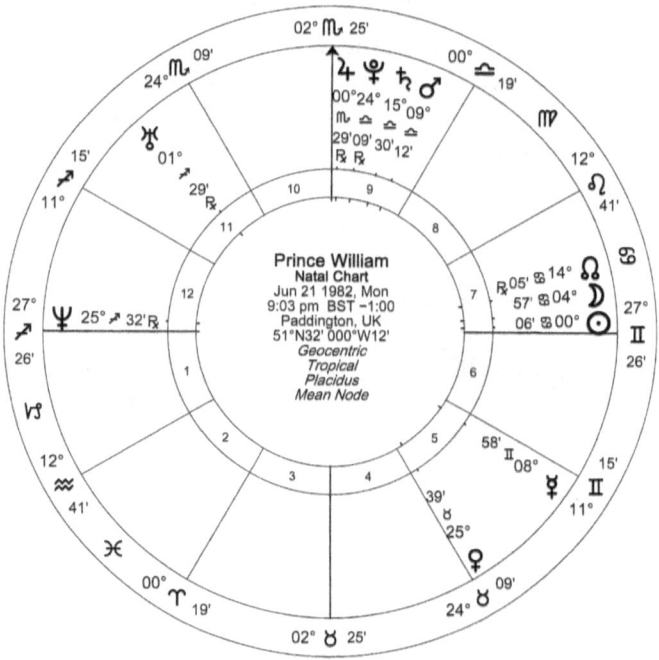

took place. He was fourteen at the time, a very vulnerable age. What was especially difficult for him would have been the disallowance a year later of the usual emotional expression which a Cancer Moon person would need for grieving. It was thoroughly internalized, and must have been very difficult to process. Chart Data: AA rating

Claude Monet

Artist Claude Monet had an exact square between the Sun and the lunar nodal axis. His mother was a singer, artistic like Claude himself, and she must have exuded what felt like physical sunshine on little Claude. Jupiter was conjunct the Sun, adding to its abundant quality. The father wanted Claude to become a grocer and help with the family business, but there was too much Sun in him for that! We could say that Monet could trust in life

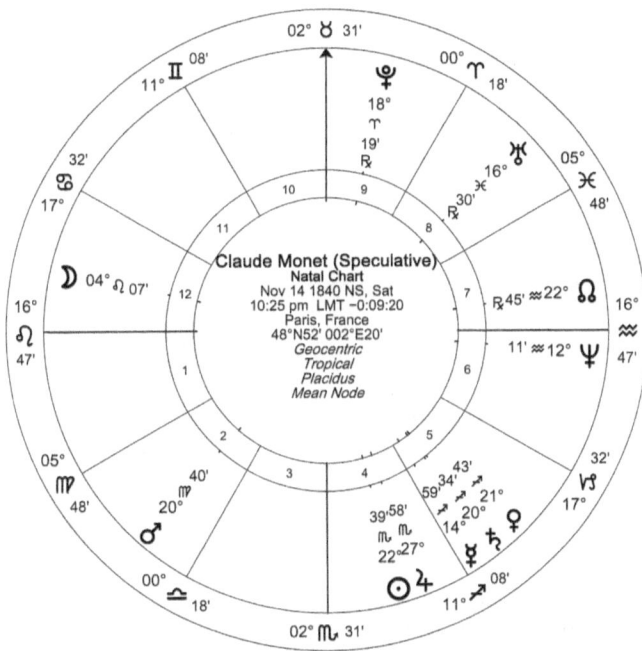

as long as he could be a beacon of light for the natural beauty around him. He rendered beautiful paintings of sunlight shining on his gardens. Perhaps he grew a few groceries there as well.

Monet's horoscope is rated X because there is no documented time. I have placed the time as an estimate for an artist, and have not rectified the time. However, we know that Monet's passion was the use of light and color, and he rendered very large paintings. As a condition of trust, he gravitated toward life in the sunshine, and to the love of home (the Sun perhaps in his fourth house). His property in Giverny, France, was a most important part of his life, very much his foundation.

David Blaine

Famed magician and stunt artist David Blaine, also with natal Sun square the lunar nodes, has often talked about how much

Emotional Dimensions of Astrology

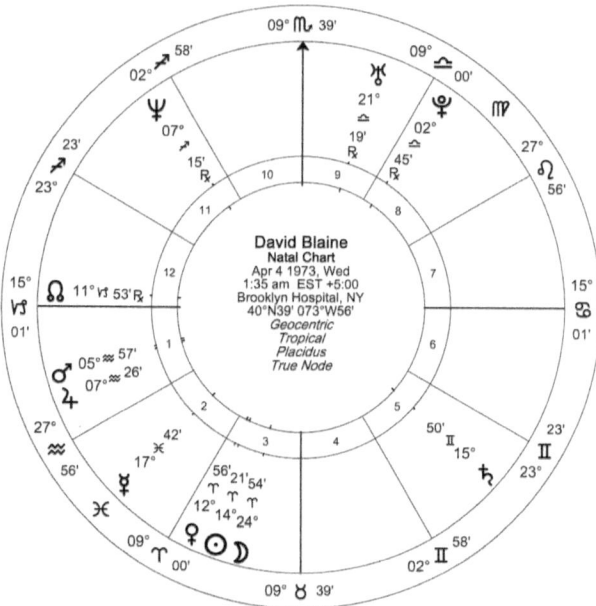

positive influence his mother had on him. He said in one interview that she gave him a pack of cards one time, and he showed her a trick he had learned. He said, "She screamed and went crazy like she'd seen the most amazing thing in the world, which it wasn't, but because of her reaction, I believed it was, so I just kept learning more and more, and started to become good at performing magic."[3]

In April 1999, when Blaine was twenty-six, and solar arc Saturn made a conjunction with the Moon's South Node in Blaine's chart, he performed his first endurance stunt, and was "buried alive" in a clear plastic coffin under tons of water, visible to the public in the street across from the Trump Tower in New York City. Blaine was reported to have said upon his release after five days of internment that he experienced a prophetic vision that all races on earth would band together in harmony. The next

---

[3]Student interview at Hallen School, November 5, 2015, on www.turnarounders.pcah.gov, retrieved December 2015.

several years, as solar arc Saturn approached the square to his Sun, Blaine developed his endurance stunts, all of which either isolated or confined him (or both).

We could say that David could trust in life as long as he can have a spotlight on himself during his very structured performances. David's time of birth is unknown, so the one shown here is speculative. It places the lunar nodal axis in the houses of confinement and discipline, and because we know he needs to perform and be on stage, it is near the Ascendant-Descendant axis. Saturn in the fifth house rules his Ascendant. Saturn is itself in a feeling realm with Mercury, so we know that David's mental discipline is an emotional situation for him, and was needed to establish his creative expression in life through mental discipline.

A statement for anyone with the nodal axis in fourth harmonic contact with the Sun could be:

> *"The suggestion is that trust in life will be present as long as there is recognition for one's worth, and a spotlight on the life of that person, not always for fun, but sometimes for very serious reasons."*

One person I know who has the Moon's nodes square the Sun and contacting Chiron was given the statement that she could trust in life as long as she could shine for others in all her misery; and she agreed that it was a pretty good description of herself. I neglected to tell her that Janis Joplin had the same aspects, but she would have especially liked hearing that since she owns a music store that features rock and roll artists.

A person who has the lunar nodes in this strong contact with the Moon was likely influenced in the early home by the mother's own appreciation for the group or the family, and even sometimes the larger family of man, and/or public work and contact in general. The sense of community, and one's place in it, would have been strong in the mother, and she passed this feeling along to the child.

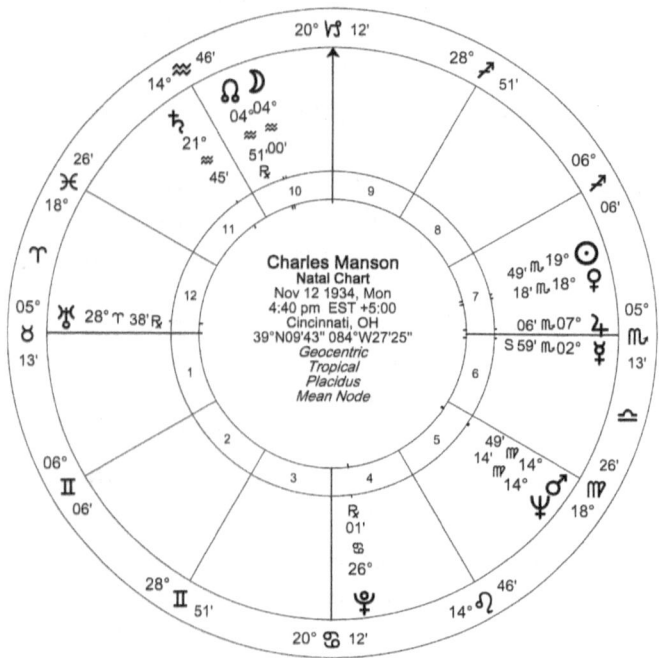

Lunar Nodes with Moon

Charles Manson

In some cases the mother's influence was a thoroughly negative manifestation, such as in the case of Charles Manson, who was partially reared by his single mother until she was incarcerated for theft. His mother depended on her group of friends and family to help her and to be her partners in crime for survival. She would pass little Charlie around her group, and ask for help caring for him.

Manson had the natal Moon conjunction the North Node in Aquarius and square a Jupiter-Mercury conjunc-

> The Moon's nodes in fourth harmonic aspect with the Moon is the need to nurture and/or represent the group in order to trust in life.

tion—a complex feeling realm that involved, for him, negative beliefs, ideas, and opinions on social injustice. After he grew up his "groupies" were women who gathered around him and helped him take out his revenge on society.

It could have been different. He could have seen how disadvantaged he had been in life and chosen to help others by fighting for justice. We could have said of Manson some years ago that he could trust in life as long as he could align himself with public causes for justice, perhaps as a rock n roll performer; but it is too late to do that now. He died November 19, 2017. Chart Data: AA Rating

Leo Buscaglia and Fred Rogers

Both Leo Buscaglia and Fred Rogers had the lunar node conjunction a Pisces Moon. Their charts are shown later in this book.

Buscaglia was an inspirational speaker called Dr. Love, and he was famous for his stories about his Italian mother and her home-made dinners that brought so many people together at the table. Her need to nurture and bring the group together was instrumental in Buscaglia's understanding of the power of love, and of caring for one another.

Mr. Rogers, of the children's tv show, spent hours with his mother and his grandfather Mr. McFeely gathering around the family piano.[4] "Gathering" is a function of the Moon, for nurturance, and gets deeply imbedded in the trust requirement. Mr. Rogers chose to have his tv show "gather" in a neighborhood, to allow them to discuss their current business of the day, and to get advice from each other.

Both Buscaglia and Rogers achieved the ultimate expressions of their creative type of Moon with lunar nodes trust in life. A general statement that can be given for someone with the lunar nodal axis in strong contact with the Moon could be:

---

[4]From Joyce DeFrancesco's article, "Remembering Fred Rogers—a life well lived." Pittsburg Magazine, April 3, 2003.

> *"The suggestion is that trust will be present in life as long as the self is given over to public concerns, for the well-being of the group, or simply to be involved in public activities."*

Lunar Nodes with Mercury

The Moon's nodes in fourth harmonic aspect with Mercury is the need to decipher and communicate in order to trust in life.

The foundation of trust for someone with Mercury in contact with the lunar nodes is the reliance and focus on mental functioning, however that might be described by sign and house position. The mother was in some way passing on the need for communication and/or mental computations in order to feel the connection with society.

Martha Washington

The figure of Martha Washington, wife of the first American president, who had the South Node conjunction Mercury in Cancer, suggests

> The Moon's nodes in fourth harmonic aspect with Mercury is the need to decipher and communicate in order to trust in life.

that her mother in the early home passed on the feeling that thinking and planning were required for trust. Martha's parents were wealthy land and slave owners, and the running of the estate must have required management that could not have been entrusted to others; so naturally the mother in the home took care of it herself. The nodes with Mercury echo Martha's Gemini Sun and stellium, which was probably in her third house. Martha married well at a young age and was widowed with children very early; she then married George Washington as he made his way up the ladder of political success. This reflects the Capricorn end of her nodal axis.

Her life, like her mother's, was based on responsibility and precise mental organization. Her faith in her own mental con-

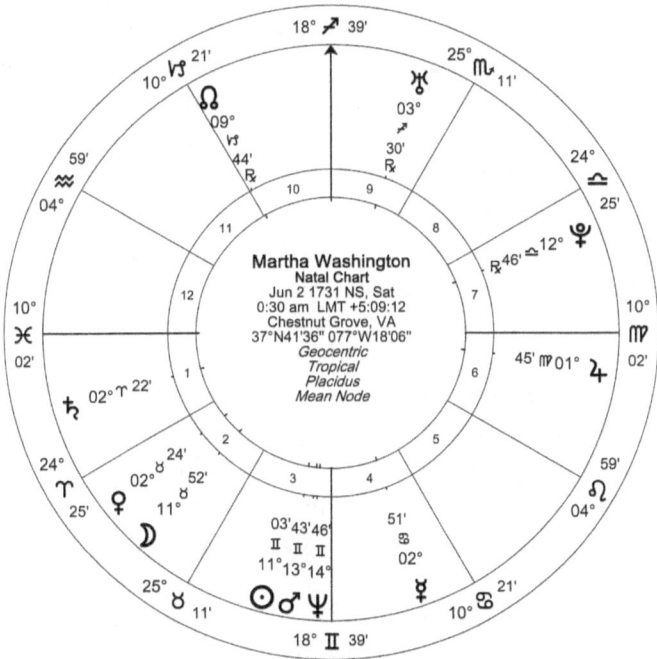

structs was her most fundamental feeling realm, even clinging to that hierarchical belief in slave ownership. With her Midheaven probably around 0 Capricorn and Saturn on her Ascendant, Martha rigidly kept the ideals her family possessed, not surprisingly. We could say that Martha could trust in life as long as her mind kept track of what was important to the security of her family. Chart Data: B Rating

Edgar Cayce

A sensitive case of a Moon's Node in contact with Mercury is that of psychic Edgar Cayce, who had Mercury in Pisces close to the nodal axis. Mercury was the closest aspect, with also a Saturn-Venus conjunction, probably in the seventh house. There are various sources for Edgar's birth time, and it is through my own rectification that I settled on the time shown here.

Emotional Dimensions of Astrology

We know very little about Cayce's mother except that she claimed to be psychic like Edgar, and she said she saw the same spirit friends that Edgar saw as a child.[5] The Saturn-Node conjunction suggests that the mother took over the role of the father in some way. We know from Cayce's own memoirs that his father was of a "coarser" material than his mother, though Edgar kindly states that his father "did the best he could."

Edgar said many times that "mind is ever the builder," insisting that the thinking function makes all the difference in our lives. Though he received information through psychic sources, and he had no control over what was shared with him during his trance states, he was never under anyone's coercion, and so he had to make up his own mind about whether there was truth or sense in it. He remained a Christian his entire life, even though he understood and accepted the premise of reincarnation.

Cayce believed that our minds are the faculty through which we ultimately decide where our emotions are going to take us. Normally Saturn close to Mercury is not easily fooled, and the function is to test everything that that is seen or heard for validity in the real world, notwithstanding that in this case it was all in Pisces. We could say that Edgar could trust in life as long as his mind could organize and build on the information that came to him from unusual sources. (Chart Data: C Rating)

A statement for a person with Mercury in strong contact with the nodes could be:

> *"The suggestion is that trust in life will be present as long as there is reliance on the mental capacity. Communication or direction is paramount to the self and others."*

Lunar Nodes with Venus

The lunar nodes in fourth harmonic aspect with Venus is the need to comply, create harmony among people, or create beauty

---

[5]From *Lost Memoirs of Edgar Cayce* (1997); see bibliography.

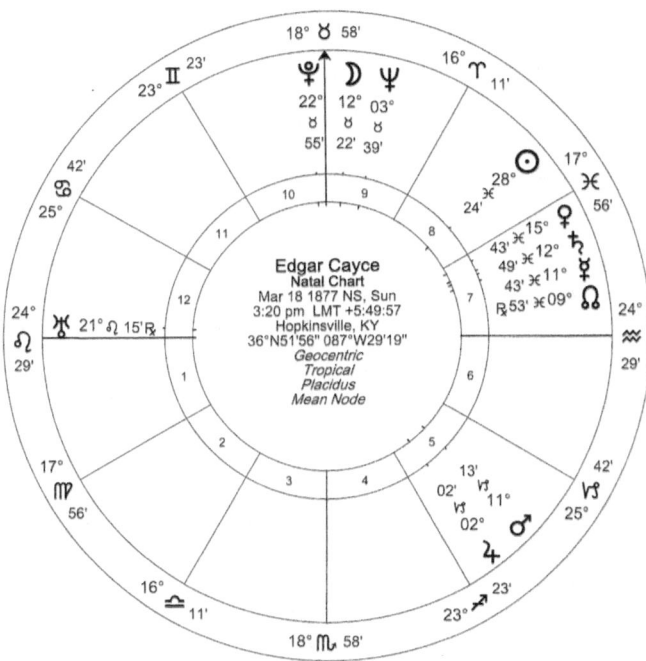

and harmony in the environment in order to trust in life.

People with Venus in these aspects to the lunar nodes will trust in life as long as they can locate the aesthetics that appeal to them. This could be engagement in harmonious relationships, creating beautiful products or environments, or simply acquiring wealth. More than any other planet, Venus' sign will suggest the kind of expression that is appropriate for the trust conditions. Someone with Venus in Taurus will be drawn toward material manifestations, such as gardening or cooking or fashion or fine art. Someone with Venus in Gemini might be drawn to books, speaking or singing. The element is instrumental.

Gordon Ramsay

Celebrity chef and restaurateur Gordon Ramsay has Venus partile and cazimi the Sun in Scorpio, so the Venus has immersed itself in the immense energy of the Sun. Accordng to Hellenistic astrologers, this increases the strength of Venus. The nodal axis is only one degree away. Gordon's passion is to build aesthetic restaurants and delectable bites, but his process for doing it is anything but compliant. He is famous for instructing others while he is throwing pots and pans and spitting out the "F" word, like a Scorpio might be expected to do.

Ramsay's mother shined favor on him as her hope in life, while she remained married to an unworthy husband. Gordon watched his mother's persistent efforts to hold together a family that was constantly being destroyed by an alcoholic, womanizing father who was also at times physically abusive to her. This story is relayed in

> **The lunar nodes in fourth harmonic aspect with Venus is the need to comply, create harmony among people, or create beauty and harmony in the environment in order to trust in life.**

his autobiography, *Humble Pie* (2008), where he paints a kind and loving picture of his mother. In addition to the lunar nodes with Venus and the Sun, we can see the rest of the story of Gordon's mother in his Virgo Moon conjunction Uranus in the fifth house, and opposition retrograde Saturn.

Ramsay's mother was a nurse (the Virgo perception he had of her), and she no doubt found creative ways to avoid and/or mend the abuse from her husband, and to bring her brand of first-aid to the family. She was Gordon's only real parent while he was growing up. In his case the compliance of Venus came with a Scorpio face and the understanding that harmony can be born out of the deepest chaos. We could say that Gordon can trust in life as long as he can bring deep transformation and healing by connecting emotionally in the workplace where good food is created. Chart Data: AA Rating

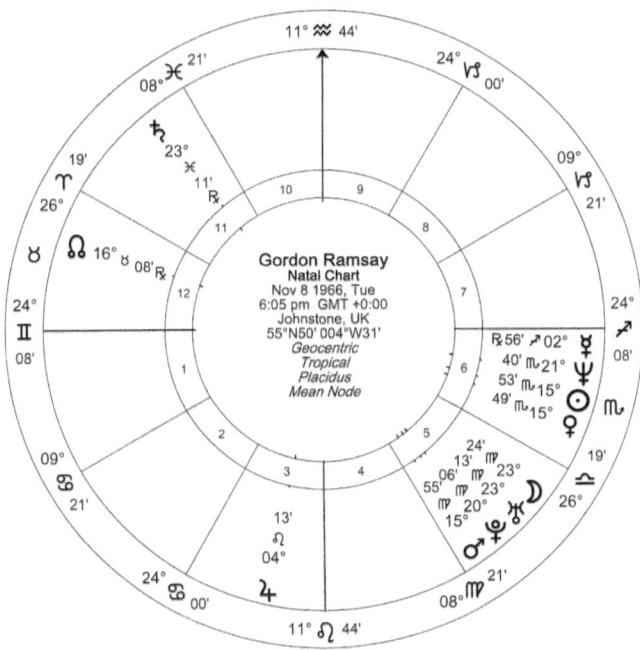

Rosa Parks

Another example of a Venus that fights passionately for harmony is Rosa Parks, who at age forty-two refused to move to the back of the bus where the "colored" people were expected to sit. Her Venus and node are in Aries. Her inner need for harmony within herself won out over the customary deference to white people, and she showed her leadership, which is how Aries always tries to express itself. This is the fabric which she was born expecting in life, the fabric her mother wove for her from her own position as a school teacher and wife who took back her dignity from an unappreciative husband.[6] We could say that Rosa could trust in life as long as she could fight to establish self-worth for herself and others.

Not everyone is aware that Rosa Parks was not simply someone who finally got tired of moving to the back of the bus. She was

Emotional Dimensions of Astrology

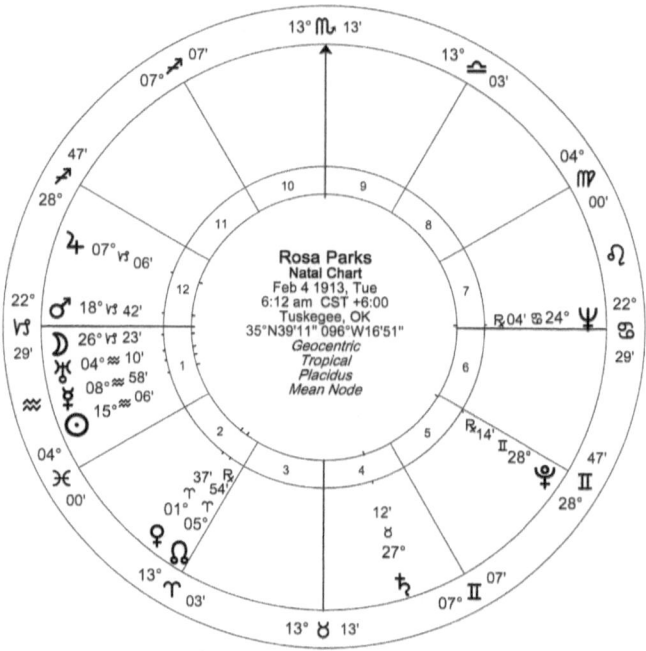

a woman who had been working in the civil rights movement for years, and had been instrumental in forming a committee for justice for a black woman, Recy Taylor, who had been gang raped by six white men. All charges against the men were dismissed even though they admitted they had raped her. Rosa's efforts for a retrial came to nothing as transiting Neptune touched her natal lunar nodes. All of the people in Alabama who had a sense of justice held their collective breaths at that time, but the men were never indicted for kidnapping and brutal rape, even though that is exactly what they had done.

It was 1955 when Rosa refused to move to the back of the bus, and in 1961, solar arc Sun came to shine on Rosa's nodal axis, as all of America watched in horror while a mob of white supremacists set fire to the Freedom Rider's bus in Alabama, and almost

---

[6] From *My Story* by Rosa Parks; see bibliography.

killed everyone in it. The Freedom Rider mission was a direct outcome of the action Rosa took when she refused to move from her seat. Public transportation in America was by constitution available to everyone, as was education and access to employment, but in reality, in 1961, it had not actualized.

Rosa is the perfect example of Venus in its greater role as worker for justice. In Rosa's case, Venus was also square Jupiter—that extra feeling realm was pushing for the right for the disempowered to expand into society and receive the social benefits guaranteed by the country's constitution.

Anyone who has Venus in strong contact with the Moon Nodes, will resonate with this statement:

> *"The suggestion is that there is trust in life as long as there is the creation of harmony or beauty or fairness in life, even if it endures chaos and disharmony in the process of acquiring it."*

Lunar Nodes with Mars

Just as a Venus person can sometimes be a fighter, a Mars person can sometimes be a peacemaker (by fighting for peace), particularly if the sign is Pisces or Libra, or if Neptune is also involved.

Terry Ryan

One of the most amusing examples of the lunar nodes with Mars is author Terry Ryan who wrote an autobiography of her years growing up in Defiance, Ohio, and named the book *The Prizewinner of Defiance Ohio* (2002). It was the story of her mother, who, at the end of the era of jingle-writing contests, was winning loads of them. Like Gordon Ramsay's mother, Terry's mother was trying to make ends meet while an alcoholic

> **The lunar nodes in fourth harmonic aspect with Mars is the need for defiance in order to trust in life.**

Emotional Dimensions of Astrology

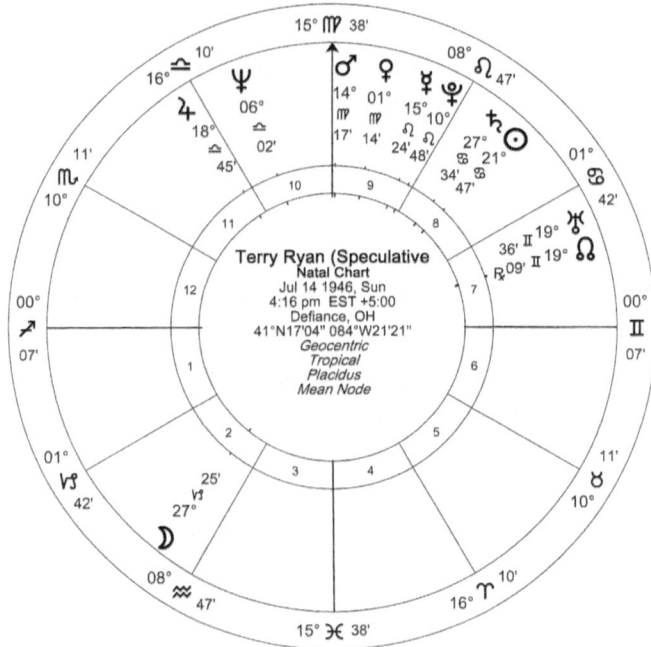

father squandered their meager income. In spite of the sad circumstances, the book is hilarious. Terry learned defiance early from her mother, a woman who refused to crumble under the constraints of a society that recommended a house full of children with no way of acquiring the means to support them.

In addition to the lunar nodes square Mars, Uranus was conjunct the North Node in Gemini. Terry was every bit as defiant as her mother, and stated that she knew by age five that she was not going to be hetero-normative. Her mother knew it too, but she let Terry find it out for herself. Terry's humor was indefatigable, one of the best qualities of the Gemini expression.

While Terri was writing the book in 2001, there was a solar arc of the Sun to her Mars, and the transiting Mars and Pluto were conjunct her nodal axis and square her natal Mars. Talk about defiance! The distance between Mars and the nodal axis in the natal chart is 6 degrees, so when Terry was six years old, there was a distinct event in her life which was simultaneously happy and tragic. As she wrote her autobiography she was pulling information from the emotional dimensions in her feeling realms and from her life. I'm sure you can spot the feeling realms in her chart. We could say to Terri that she can trust in life as long as she can stand up for herself and others responsibly and quietly without causing more damage than has already occurred. Throughout her book she described her father with compassion, accepting his place in their family even though he failed them completely. Chart Data: Speculative

Edward Snowden

Whistleblower Edward Snowden took it upon himself to disclose high security information from the NSA (U.S. National Security Administration). The act of disclosure was defiance, and many people believe that he had good reasons for doing it.

Possibly the most telling factor is the presence of Mars in Gemini closely conjunction the nodal axis, with Neptune in the opposite position with the node. Aside from what it might mean for Snowden, it screams "taking information from those who keep it hidden." We know little about his mother. She served as chief deputy in a district court, a job that put her in the center of privileged information. Edward's chart has a Scorpio Moon in the sixth house, representing his perception of his mother as both in control and having the need to keep confidentiality in her position at work.

Snowden overstepped normal and high-security boundaries to access information that in his opinion was unfairly acquired. The whole story requires the whole horoscope, and an analysis of the Moon square Venus as well as the Sun opposition Neptune, and of course the facts of the case. By itself, the nodal picture describes a social construct whereby Snowden can trust in life, as he finds himself in places where information is kept secret. There

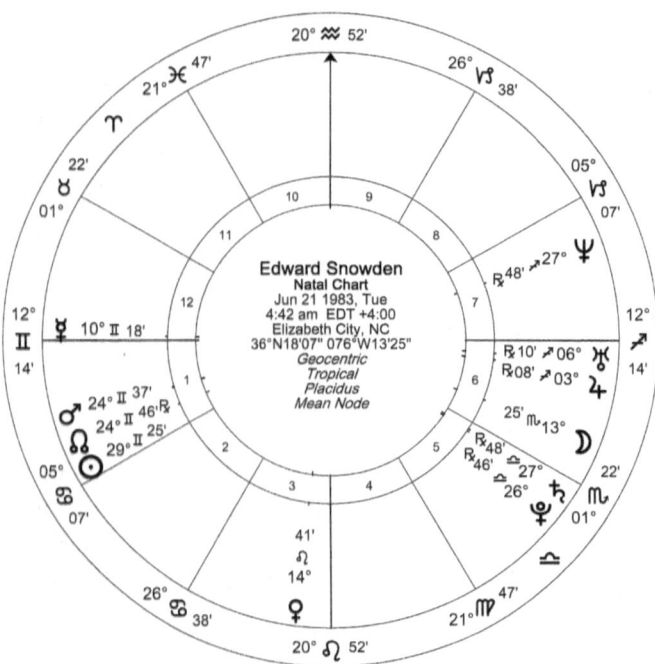

has always been a need for secret information in this world, and/or for it to be exposed. Whether it is right is a different story. Chart Data: AA Rating

We can give someone with Mars in the fourth harmonic to the lunar nodes a statement such as this:

> *"You can trust in life as long as you have a cause that you are fighting for, of if you have found a niche where you can be the initiator of action where action is required for the common good."*

Lunar Nodes with Jupiter

Jupiter energy is often related to magnification, or making mountains out of molehills. Many celebrities have this aspect and express it in a physical way. Jupiter is also related to a perspective that is broad, and to liberal justice in general, as opposed

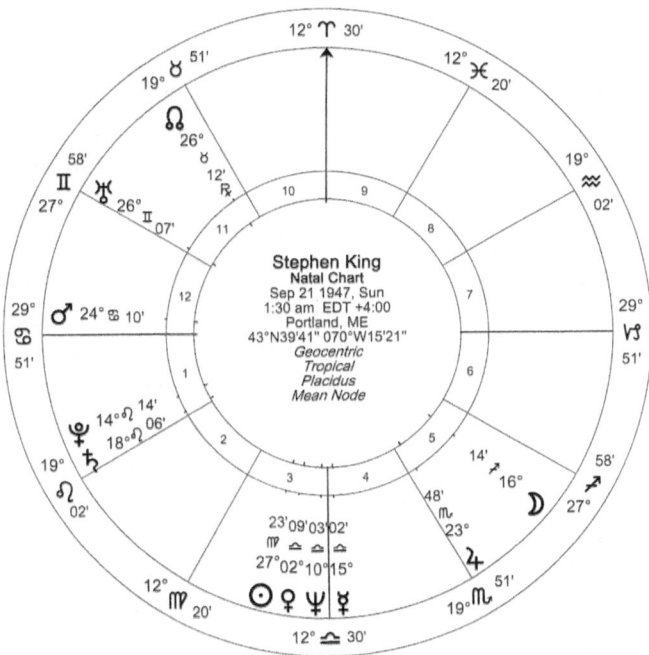

to Saturnian restrictions. These are rather varying expressions of Jupiter, but they can operate together, such as when celebrities join political movements; or it can be purely physical, such as is seen with some athletes. Sign and house positions will help us with the nature of the expression.

> Lunar nodes in fourth harmonic aspect with Jupiter is the need for expansion and largesse in order to trust in life.

The mother in the early home passed on the need to have some sort of exaggeration or an expanded picture. Without being in these situations in life, nothing would feel right. There was the need for the big picture to appear through the mother, something bigger than real life, inspiring, and possibly funny.

Emotional Dimensions of Astrology

Stephen King

Author Stephen King has Jupiter in Scorpio conjunction the South Node. When Stephen was age two his father left the family and never returned. Being a merchant seaman, the father had never really been with the family in the first place. His mother was all that Stephen ever had. Jupiter and the South Node are also square Saturn, and Pluto by a distance.

This is a complex feeling realm, and of course it has everything to do with King's grand and exaggerated sense of the macabre. We can say that Stephen can trust in life as long as he can be creative in an over-the-top way to express Saturn and Pluto stories.

Stephen's Moon in Sagittarius (his perception of his mother) echoes the Jupiter message that she offered him. His mother was religious, according to Stephen, but she also had a quick and quirky mind, which we see in her own Uranus-Mercury conjunction in Aquarius. In Stephen's book *On writing: a Memoir of the Craft* (2001) he calls his mother "self-sufficient, funny, and slightly nutty." He recalls that in the second grade when he had a teacher who had "Bride of Frankenstein" hair and protruding eyes, his mother once said of her, "When Mrs. Taylor and I are talking I always want to cup my hands under her peepers in case they fall out!" Now that is hyperbole, and very funny! Chart Data: A Rating

Steffi Graf

Steffi Graf, a Jupiter-lunar node person, is a champion tennis player and considered the all-time most accomplished female tennis player in the world. She is not known for her humor, but there were many superlatives in her career. Jupiter is the closest in conjunction to her nodal axis, and Pluto and Uranus are also closely conjunct, adding tremendous desire for improvement and reform. Steffi's Sun is square the nodal axis so we know that her mother's hopes for her were enormous, perhaps to replace the hopes that did not pan out in her own life. The Ascendant is also involved.

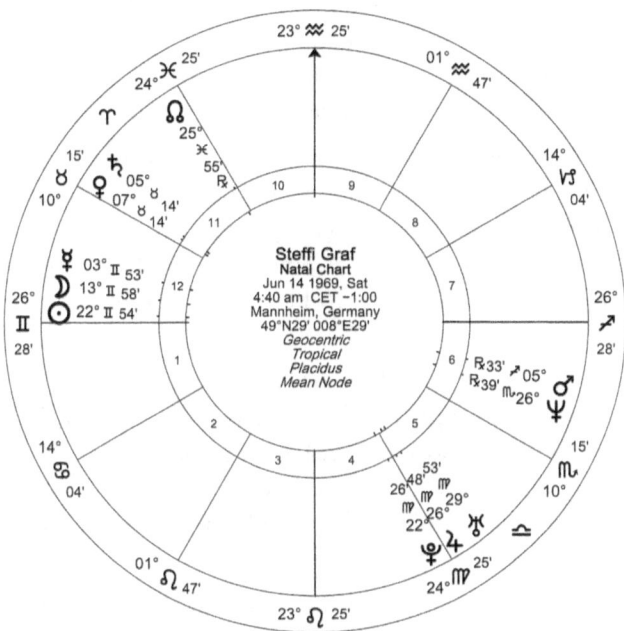

Heidi Graf, Steffi's mother, has a Saturn-Mars conjunction that is conjunct Steffi's Sun (and of course square the Jupiter set). This reflects an extremely complex relationship between them with hints of tremendous pressure on Steffi to succeed in order to please her mother.

Heidi's own nodal axis is conjunct Pluto, and the set is square to Steffi's Venus-Saturn pair. Already we are traveling deep into their family psyche which is too involved for comfort; yet it is the Jupiter energy that resounds so prominently. It is the path which was so familiar to Steffi and to her fans.

Her father, Peter Graf (b. June 18, 1938), was the one who pushed and trained Steffi from a very young age. He has a close nodal conjunction with Steffi's Neptune, while his Neptune is conjunct her Pluto.[7] This is all to say that her family ties are very

---

[7] At Peter's death, from *Los Angeles Times*, December 6, 2013, "Passings: Peter Graf, father of tennis great was jailed for tax fraud."

Emotional Dimensions of Astrology

intense, each person connected to the emotional dimensions of the other. We can say that the Jupiter energy was a prime energy in her life because her family expected so much from her, and always wanted things to be bigger and better than they already were.

Many factors were involved with the lunar Nodes, but the father was not left out of the picture. Though this is a complex chart, even without parents who pushed her to the extreme, Steffi could only trust in life as long as she pushed herself hard to perform well in her craft, to be a star, to be on stage, to be the best.

Now that she has retired from her tennis career, Steffi donates time to her non-profit foundation called Children for Tomorrow, for children who have been traumatized. This is the generalized liberal justice mentioned above. We might wonder if Steffi herself was traumatized by the intense pressure to win at all costs. Chart Data: AA Rating

Any person who has Jupiter in contact with the nodes might be told:

> *"The suggestion is that there will be trust in life as long as there is exaggeration, or hope and pursuit of expansion, especially if it is accompanied through enjoyment, and even while working hard for it."*

In the two cases above we can easily see the superlatives of Jupiter. Stephen King writes every day for six hours, and he has written more than 120 books. He is prodigious—a good word for Jupiter. Steffi Graf is the top-ranked tennis player of all time, not because she is the absolute best at every aspect of it but because of her continual force for improvement and her multitude of wins. She is, like Stephen King, prodigious. Jupiter, like the sign Sagittarius, wishes to inspire, and to live in joy. That is the positive expression of Jupiter.

Lunar Nodes with Saturn

Important aspects with Saturn suggest that the mother was required to take on the role of the father, either because of his weakness or absence, or because of the perceived inadequacy of the father's role as father. In these cases it was the woman in the early home who made the rules and decisions, or provided criticism. Sometimes it is more subtle than that, such as when the mother constantly alliterates what the father would expect from the children, appearing to hide behind the father's rules, or is just stepping forward when he cannot be there.

W.B. Yeats

One would expect the Irish poet William Butler Yeats, who was interested his whole life in metaphysics and the occult, to have his Moon Nodes at birth in strong aspect to say, Neptune or Mercury in Pisces. But Yeats had the nodal axis at Libra-Aries and conjunct to Saturn in the eighth house). The eighth house does at least resonate with what we know of Yeats, with his interest in alternative subjects and the occult.

> **Lunar nodes in fourth harmonic aspect with Saturn is the need to bring order and criticism into contacts with others, in order to have trust.**

William's mother, Susan, had a reputation for being very angry about her marriage. Her husband John was a failed businessman turned artist, a man who was not able to keep up with the family expenses.[8] Susan (b. Jul 13, 1841) had a Mercury-Neptune opposition conjunct to her own natal Moon nodes, thus corroborating her need to live in artistic fantasy, and dramatize the Irish faerie stories to her children, which Yeats said she did. Yet she also had a Sun-Mars-Pluto T-square, so we know that there were turbulent feelings surrounding the male archetype within her (and with her husband).

---

[8]From *Geography of the Imagination*; see bibliography.

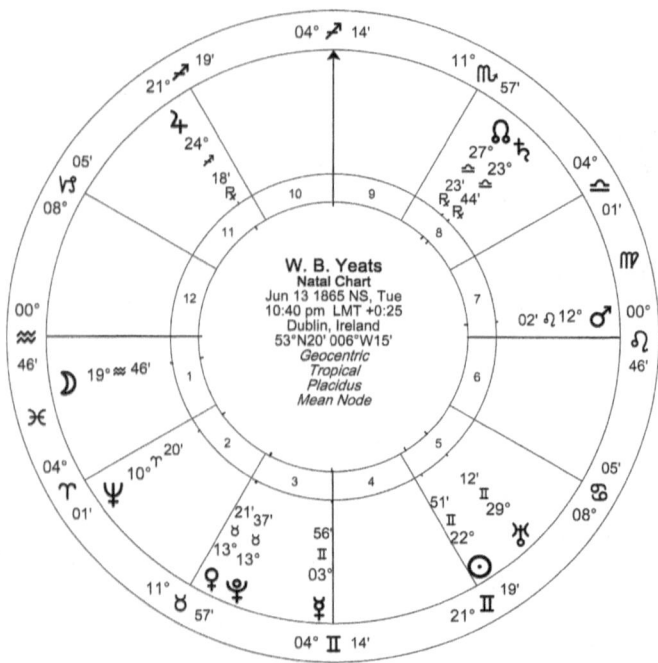

That William came into this life with a lunar node in the eighth house certainly speaks of his mother's preoccupation with financial debt (who knows if she could remedy any of it), so we cannot discard that the Saturn might represent his mother's feelings of poverty and strife—the limitations in life. Yeats, however, chose to concentrate on the preservation of the wealth of Irish storytelling, and he created a foundation in Ireland and a building in which to house them. The eighth house can refer to heritage or legacy. Whatever wealth Yeats' mother felt was taken from her, Yeats protected the wealth he thought was important to her and to him—her stories, Ireland's stories.

This example of Yeats is important to remember when we see a lunar Node condition in someone's chart and we make a word picture of it that does not resonate well with that person. There are numerous ways in which these conditions will be passed on from mother to child. It is our job as astrologers to seek out the

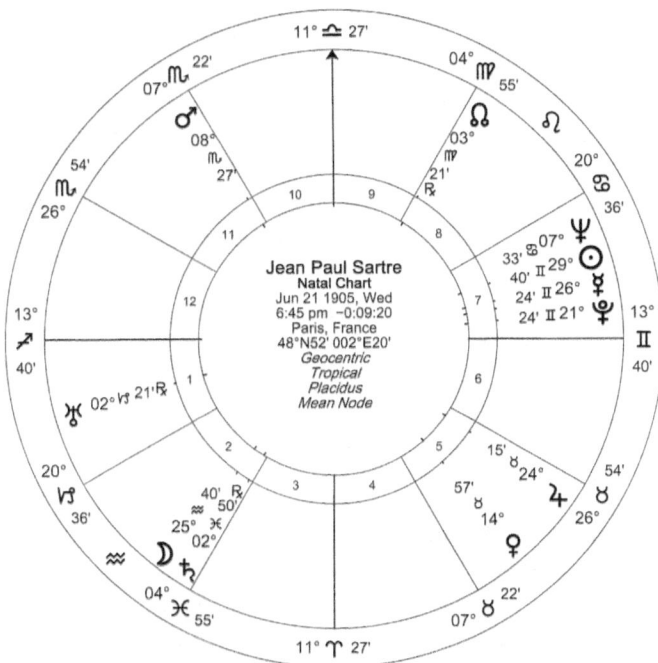

way in which it is best described. In Yeats' case, we would have needed to ask him about the Saturn restriction or criticism coming from the mother. We could tell Yeats that he could trust in life as long as he was constructing a safe place for what was of shared value to him in life. Chart Data: AA Rating

Jean Paul Sartre

Surprisingly, another person with Saturn conjunction the South Node was the existentialist philosopher and writer Jean Paul Sartre. His core beliefs were centered on the idea that people deal with an abundance of choices in life, but that a person's life is only meaningful if it is authentically lived and not necessarily in line with societal constrictions. Sartre's philosophy was that since there is no proof of any ultimate authority (the Saturn symbol!) and that our freedom is only limited by the freedom of others, that all other actions are allowed. It's not a very original philosophy, but certainly Virgo-Pisces, full of references to freedom of expression.

In Sartre's horoscope Saturn is in Pisces in the third house. Repeating that theme of communications is the stellium with the Sun in Gemini. Jean Paul's life was not so much about freedom of action as it was about freedom of thought. His father died when he was a toddler, so he never really knew his father. He was close to his mother and he loved talking with her. He objected to her remarrying when he was age twelve, and so he was sent away to boarding school to get him out of the way.[9] At age twelve his lunar nodal axis made a solar arc to square his Ascendant-Descendant axis. It must have been difficult for him that his mother chose a new husband at that time over being solely with him.

Sartre loved freedom, but he knew that freedom must be defined, which is why he wrote *Nausea*, in which he describes the shocking encounter between self and free will, where the hero awakens to find that he is living his life as if it were a script, as if it were fated. Sartre discovered that his life had meaning if he chose to create the meaning for himself—a wonderful description of Saturn in Pisces with the lunar nodes. We could say of Sartre that he could trust in life as long as he could contemplate and talk with others about whether humans could construct their own freedom. Chart Data: AA Rating; his charat is shown in a later chapter.

People who are born with Saturn conjunction or square the lunar nodal axis can be told:

> "The suggestion is that there will be trust in life as long as there is a foundation created which has a structure, even if it means confinement and criticism, so that everything else can be free."

---

[9]From *Jean Paul Sartre*; see bibliography.

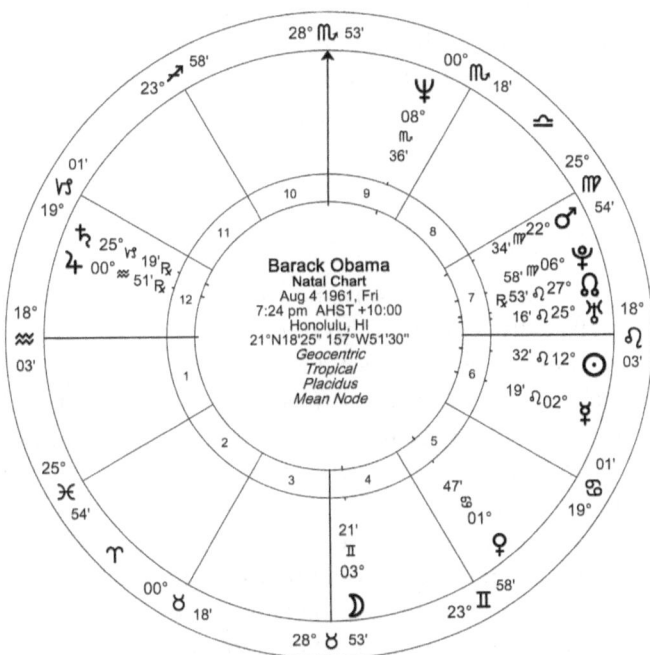

Lunar Nodes with Uranus

When Uranus is in strong contact with the lunar nodes, the mother in the early home insisted on a special identity for the child, which is not quite the same as the nodes in contact with the Sun discussed above. It is not so much about fame, but about uniqueness. The mother recognized or instilled some special spark in the child. Sometimes that spark might take away from the mother's own unique qualities, and so she tries to steal it back. This is similar to what happens when a girl becomes a teenager, and the mother is reminded of her lost youth.

> **Lunar nodes in fourth harmonic aspect with Uranus is the need to be special in order to trust in life.**

---

[10] Article by Tim Jones, "Barack Obama: mother not just a girl from Kansas," Chicago Tribune, April 2, 20212.

Emotional Dimensions of Astrology 53

If a child's individuality is stolen or used by the mother for her own purposes (taking credit for it), it is a sad thing. But if the mother is wisely challenging her child to be as unique as is safely possible, then all is good. In either case it can have the same effect of encouraging the child to develop some stand-out qualities.

Barack Obama

Barack Obama has the lunar nodal axis conjunction Uranus in Leo. His mother, who was his single parent, had a great influence on him.[10] She was a well-known academic radical white activist in college, and appeared to be attracted to men of foreign heritage, especially those who were anti-colonial revolutionary. When Barack was born, to say that Stanley Dunham had hopes for him to fulfill her idealism would not be incorrect. Since Barack was a person of color, he was perfectly suited to fulfill her dreams. In some respects, it could be said to be robbing Barack's identity for her own cause. But perhaps Barack would not have wanted it any other way. We could say that by the suggestion of the lunar nodal situation that Obama can trust in life as long as he can maintain a special recognition for himself. This, of course, has already been accomplished in perpetuity.

African-American people in the U.S. who were directly descended from slavery in this country (Obama's heritage was colonially controlled territories in Africa) hadn't yet provided an individual for the office of the presidency of the United States. If Obama's mother was hoping that her son would be the first one, he was hoping for it as well. He said as much in his book, *Dreams from my Father*.

Living as if you are special is how all lunar node-Uranus people live. It is not so much about achieving a special recognition as about living as a unique person, being "one of a kind." There are indeed other presidents with this configuration. Presidents George W. Bush and Bill Clinton both have Uranus in Gemini

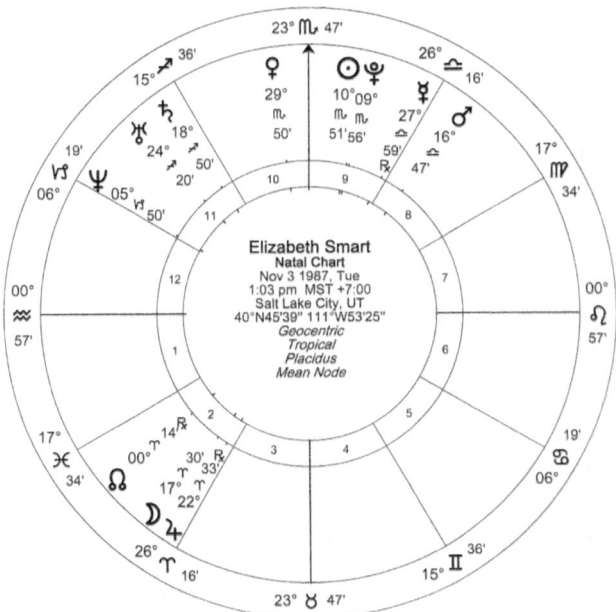

conjunction the Moon Nodal axis. They both have unique ways of talking, Bill with his lingering drawl, and George with his funny word errors. Chart Data: AA Rating

Those who have Uranus in strong contact with the lunar nodal axis, can be told:

> "The suggestion here is that there is trust in life as long as there is the acceptance of being unique, having an appreciation for it, and being allowed the sense of separation from others because of a distinction and/or need for adventure."

Lunar Nodes with Neptune

Neptune with the lunar nodal axis in strong aspect suggests that the mother in the early home was immersed in idealism, or was spiritually or artistically motivated, or negatively, had departed from reality because it did not meet the ideal. There is a broad spectrum of expression, including drug use, victimization, or, conversely, working hard for a better reality.

Elizabeth Smart

At age fourteen, Elizabeth Smart was kidnapped from her home by a homeless man whom her family had briefly employed to work in their yard. Elizabeth's father didn't need to avoid paying for a landscaper as the family was financially successful; he simply wanted to be kind, so he hired an indigent person. Elizabeth was a victim of this accidental exposure to evil. Her lunar nodes at the Aries point are square Neptune, and are in the second and eighth houses of self-esteem and the values of others.

> The lunar nodes in fourth harmonic aspect with Neptune is the need to be unified with others in spiritual or artistic or self-sacrificing ways.

Neptune is so often about victimization because the function of Neptune is to include rather than to exclude, and that requires a well-functioning Saturn to establish boundaries. One way or another, Elizabeth would be exposed to some of the lowest levels of human degradation in life, as might be expected from a Sun-Pluto conjunciton in Scorpio. Used in a positive environment, such a person might be employed in law enforcement. But even that would not protect a person from the emotional consequences of the proximity to evil. Fate, if it exists, seems to be more pronounceable in childhood, but Elizabeth's destiny was to help other victims, which she continues to do.

The most striking thing about the story of Elizabeth is that she did not just disappear from the world after she was found and saved. As a captive she had undergone extreme trauma for months, but after a recovery time, her focus was on how other people registered her not as a person but as a victim. She declared many times that she had to endure the glances from people who considered her to be "damaged goods."

This is the theme of her lunar nodes in the second and eighth houses, and it is strongly linked to her Neptune, which rules the second house, the house of self-value. She refused to be a victim, and she began a campaign to help bridge the gap between survivors like herself and the general public. I don't even need to speak with Elizabeth to see that she is a whole person today, not in spite of what happened to her but because of it.

Her desire was to give back to the world what was supposedly taken from her—her own dignity. She proved that no one, except ourselves, can take our dignity away. We could say of Elizabeth Smart that she can trust in life as long as she can be a leader for self-esteem, especially for those who have had their boundaries compromised. Chart Data: A Rating

Florence Nightingale

Who in history but Florence Nightingale would be the poster child for Neptunian self-sacrifice? Her lunar nodes were square Neptune, and at the Aries Point in Capricorn, the preferred sign for many scientific minds.

Florence was the first person to be a registered nurse and she established the profession of nursing by identifying the need for it.

Since we have no documented time for her birth, I created a chart that most effectively represents who she was, someone who took on the responsibility of providing proper care for people. This places the lunar nodes at the Midheaven. It must be considered speculative, but there is no harm in taking a look. Neptune was kept company that day by both Uranus and Pluto near the lunar nodes, and so we see that Florence was suited to overturn the whole medical system by stepping up and showing what should and could be done.

We can wonder what else was compelling for Florence that she sacrificed herself so greatly for others. That is a complex study that wanders into her emotional dimension of Saturn square Ve-

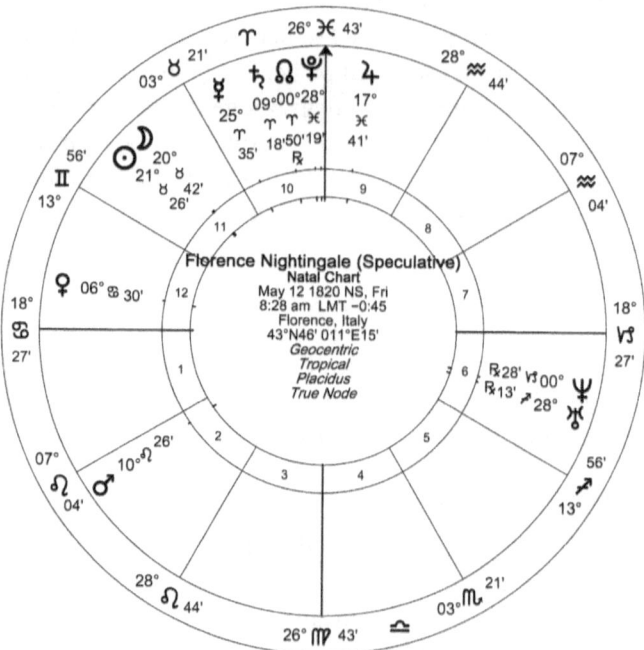

nus, I believe. She never married. Her sense of personal lovability might have been very complex, perhaps something like that of Mother Theresa, who also had Saturn square Venus. What we do know is that Neptune manifested as her complete dedication to the healing of others, so we could say that Florence could trust in life as long as she sacrificed her own needs for the love and healing of others.

We could say to a person with lunar nodes in hard aspect to Neptune:

> *"You can trust in life as long as you can find the unifying principle which brings people together. It might be in the art which you create, your spiritual work, or your dedication of your work for others."*

Unfortunately, for many, the unifying principle is a base level of eradicating the pain and suffering from their lives, such as with alcohol or heroin. Addiction to anything that brings a feeling of utopia for the sake of the feeling only is not the highest expression of Neptune energy, although some addictions can be said to be harmless (such as video games). Chart Data: Speculative.

Lunar Nodes with Pluto

Pluto can manifest on deeply divergent levels. Uranus is a focal point, Neptune is wide, and Pluto is deep. When the Moon's nodes are with Pluto, the mother in the early home was very tightly tied with the inner feelings of the child. To me, this is only ok if there is some circumstance in the family that requires this invasive sort of protection. Otherwise, it is just the need to control. It could result in never letting children experience their own feelings by themselves. Since freedom of experience is an essential part of growing up, this could be an extremely damaging aspect if the mother does not reign in her control.

> The lunar nodes in fourth harmonic aspect with Pluto is the need to go deeply to find underlying motives, in order to trust in life.

Jeffrey Green, in his book on Pluto, says that Pluto correlates to the soul (*The Evolutionary Journey of the Soul*, Volume I, p.1). I think the definition is far reaching, and can leave some of us bewildered, although his book is meaningful for many. I believe the entire horoscope is the soul. Some people are just not going to go Pluto deep. Pluto represents the area in our life where we delve most deeply for some hidden truth that holds our fascination; but Pluto is no more the soul than what is described by Neptune. In fact, since Neptune is more unifying, we are more likely to discover "soul" by being part of the collective, and at one with the universe or the creator. Uranus, too, in its insistence on uniqueness, suggests awareness of individuality living within the collective, which can be an awe-inspiring phenomenon. All of these variations allow us to get in touch with soul, something not always accomplished

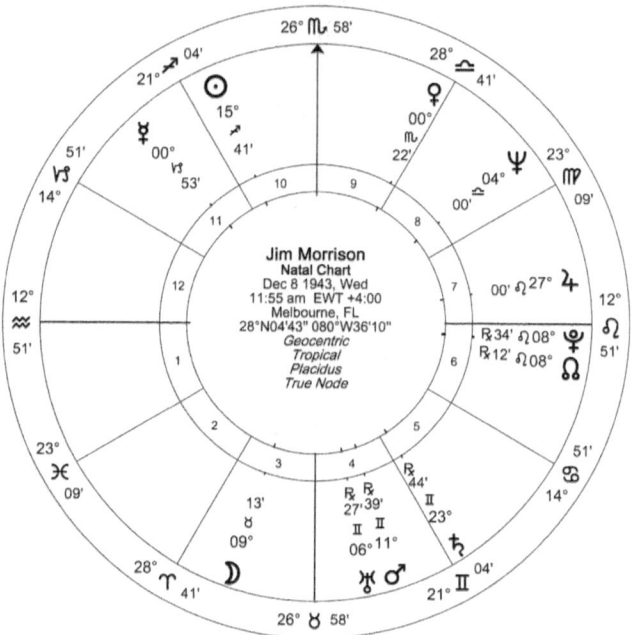

by the function of Pluto.

If a person with Pluto and the lunar nodes in strong contact does not have the feeling of control in his or her life, the foundation of trust will involve spending energy maintaining personal power and wasting energy undermining the power of others, especially through emotional manipulation of others. If a girl feels that her mother is vying for attention with her, there is a tremendous amount of pressure to become a person in control, something her mother brought to the picture in the home. If a boy feels overwhelmed by his mother and made to feel small, he feels a tremendous amount of pressure to be his own boss some day. Astrologers must ask and wait for the person to clarify the picture for us. How was the mother dominant? How was her breathing space interfering with the child's breathing space?

Jim Morrison

One Pluto person was rock star Jim Morrison, who is still seen today as one of the all-time famous lead rock singers in history; he died in 1971. Obviously Jim had little or no control over himself because he died of a drug overdose before age thirty, at the height of his success. He had in his teenage years dabbled in dark metaphysics and drugs, letting his mind go deep into experimental questions about life and the more esoteric management of it.

Journalist Jerry Hopkins, who had a long-time relationship with Jim and wrote three biographies about him, recorded Jim Morrison's brother Andy as saying that their mother colluded with the military father for military-like control over the children. Andy stated that the parenting was formulated to humiliate and verbally abuse the children for any waywardness, just like an old-school drill sergeant would have done.

Morrison's Sun is opposition Saturn, and the Moon is square the North Node-Pluto conjunction. It is quite sad to read about the mistreatment he suffered. The Taurus Moon, which, if it were by itself, could suggest a mother who loved baking cookies for her children, but in this horoscope is confounded by a mother who wanted excessive emotional control over her children.

Confirmation that the parenting was exactly as Morrison's brother said it was is seen in the parental axis in his chart, the Midheaven-Nadir axis, ruled by Pluto and Venus. Venus, as well, is in the nodal axis with Pluto, and with the Moon. The parenting was indeed smothering, claustrophobic, and overpowering. This of course is the negative expression of it, but we have no reason to doubt the circumstances because we know the outcome.

In Morrison's case, the Pluto contact with the Nodes is also conjunct the Ascendant-Descendant axis, so his need was to represent on stage the pressure that was on the whole social group of his generation. He was the poster child for this difficult energy. His death no doubt left many fans feeling more lost than they

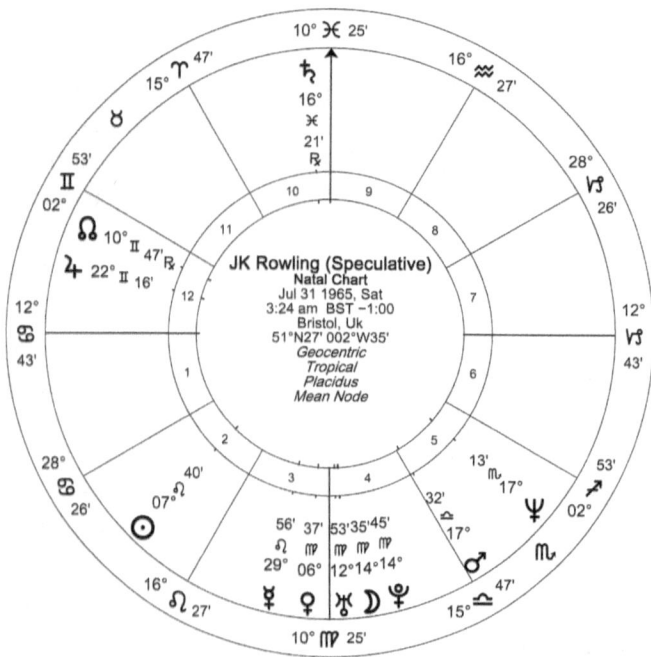

had been, along with his girlfriend Pamela Courson. Her death soon followed his. Both of their lives were very short and intense, and they had many similarities in their charts and in their lives. Chart Data: A Rating

Joanne (J.K.) Rowling

A happier outcome of a Pluto contact with the lunar nodes can be seen in the life of author J.K. Rowling, who has an extremely busy lunar nodal situation. This is appropriate for her because there are a multitude of characters in the Harry Potter series resembling her lunar node feeling realm. Instead of manifesting her lunar nodal situation in the world at large, she did it in her creative world of characters. (This chart is speculative as no time is available.)

Joanne's lunar nodes are at 12 Gemini-Sagittarius, and Uranus is at 12 Virgo 54, less than one degree from an exact square.

Uranus is closely conjunct Pluto at 14 Virgo 46, and in addition, Saturn is at 16 Pisces 21, opposite them. These are very close aspects, and because of the Pluto-Uranus-Saturn connection, they are heavily generational. I have placed her Moon at 17 Virgo 43, through my own rectification, suggesting the very personal nature of all of it for her. This would be why so many people relate to her stories, though I cannot be 100 percent sure of her birth time. Chart Data: Speculative

This all forms a grand cross of energy in her chart. If we pull apart some of the strands, we can say that the mother in the family was required to take on the role of the father for Joanne (Saturn), and impart to her child the reality that life is filled with drama, shock, and then hopefully reconstruction. The Pluto in the picture is usually considered to be the darkest energy. J.K.'s character Voldemort is certainly dark, and very central to her work of fiction.

J.K.'s father was an aircraft engineer, away from home a lot, and according to J.K., was not emotionally available. The Sun in her chart makes no ptolemaic aspects, suggesting that the father was isolated from her.[11] Her mother's situation was intense. She was diagnosed with multiple sclerosis when Joanne was fifteen, although she continued to be a working mother. At age fifteen, Joanne's Mercury was making a solar arc conjunction to Pluto, awakening her to the lunar node situation. She trusted that life consisted of great drama, and required great action and bravery.

Without speaking with J.K., it would be impossible to know how that played out in the home, but J.K. has said that her mother's influence was great. She watched her mother battle her disease for ten years. Perhaps she watched her mother grow in wisdom as they worked through their emotional dimensions and sought to learn from each other. Rather than being in competition with her mother for love from the father (maybe initially), it

---

[11] Ian Parker's article, "Mugglemarch: J.K. Rowling Writes a Realistic Novel for Adults," *The New Yorker*, October 1, 2012.

became an epic story of soul growth for them both. We could say that J.K. could trust in life as long as she could take on responsibility for others (lunar nodes with Midheaven), to refine and define the drama and transformation that takes place in our lives.

Harry Potter fans will recognize the dark Pluto energy in her books, the victory over death, and the need to vanquish Voldemort's hatred. The mythology that J.K. created in the Harry Potter series was a reflection of the inner saga she experienced in her home, and later out in her world.

For someone with Pluto in strong contact with the lunar nodal axis, we could say:

> *"The suggestion is that there will be trust in life as long as there is the ability to delve into the most difficult emotional questions, and search for the answers there, both for self-understanding, and to understand the emotional complexes of others."*

It does seem that Pluto contacts will bring the strongest emotional intensity and discoveries when placed with the lunar nodes. That is what Jeffrey Green was talking about. Just as in all of the fourth harmonic aspects, the challenge is to go deep into the most turbulent possibilities in life in order to bring about the most powerful transformation possible.

Chapter 3

Making Word Pictures

> *"You must know that there is nothing higher and stronger and more wholesome and good for life in the future than some good memory, especially a memory of childhood, of home. People talk to you a great deal about your education, but some good, sacred memory, preserved from childhood, is perhaps the best education. If a man carries many such memories with him into life, he is safe to the end of his days, and if one has only one good memory left in one's heart, even that may sometime be the means of saving us."—The Brothers Karamazov*

In the last chapter, the descriptions of the lunar nodal axes were simple and did not include anything about the ruling planets of either of the nodes. It would be enough, to start with, to just look at the signs of the nodes and the houses in which they reside to form a description of the trust situation. This is different from the process we will use for looking at the other fourth harmonic aspects, which require more discussion with the individual. For a trust profile, the primary feeling realm, we want to offer a person a simple statement to be remembered and to be referred to later in the discussion.

A simple example of this is a lunar nodal axis in the third and ninth houses in Gemini and Sagittarius. We could say to that person, "You can trust in life as long as you can engage in communication on a grand scale, and share your ideas." This may or may not have anything to do with the person's career; it is just a required condition.

Also, as stated earlier, although sextiles and trines can be part of the nodal description, my advice is to ignore other measurements and focus on the fourth harmonic ones for the purposes of this book. If you are familiar with special case measurements such as the quindecile, you might know that they can bring striking messages; but since the quindecile is not a measurement that builds in the way hard aspects do, I am foregoing it here to bring everything down to basics. I won't mention semi-squares either, or sesqui-quadrates, though they too can add something to the picture.

It is really just a matter of finding what works most efficiently. Keeping a process to a minimum is best if it works. It is too easy to get lost in a horoscope and start spinning around with lots of different ideas that do not coalesce very well. Synthesis is what we want. The reason we look at the nodal axis with fewer steps than we do with the other feeling realms is because the nodal situation is a trust condition only, and not a function in our lives. If there is more than one planet involved with the lunar nodes, then that increases the complexity of it, and we have to treat it as an extraordinary need. There will be specific examples of this later.

The process of identifying and describing feeling realms in the chart which are not the lunar nodes begins with the functions of the planets, and secondly, the houses those planets rule. The houses in which the planets live are less integral to our process here. Like lunar nodes, the houses are not functions; they are areas of development—and, in this book, we are considering how we feel about those areas. When you identify the tension between the planets, you are identifying the tension between different functions in life. There is tension between the houses the planets rule.

The best way to handle all of this if you are a beginner and you see that there are more than two planets in fourth harmonic aspect, is to slow down and take it step by step. Take each planet in relation to the other, one by one, and then after that, you can "bundle" some of them together—the ones that seem to say something important when they are all in a relationship. It is a process, and allows for individual creativity from the astrologer.

Try not to emphasize the meaning of the houses in which the planets reside. Keep your emphasis on the houses they rule. For a humanistic astrologer, the understanding is that the houses that are ruled are the ones that will relate to early development, and because of that, they will carry the emotional stamp. At first, don't even emphasize the zodiac sign of the planet (the type of expression) until you are confident that you have defined the tension between the functions.

There are lots of books with general descriptions about the hard aspects, but they are not usually framed within the construct of how we feel about them. For Mercury in hard aspect with Saturn, for instance, there will be descriptions that suggest the tendency to have a strict form of communication, or a conventional approach to thinking, etc.; but most descriptions will neglect to discuss the deep emotional concern there is for making a mental error, or how much angst there is about constructing properly framed ideas, let alone being responsible for every single word. What we want is to find out what in particular in the life is affected so strongly by this sensitivity, where it came from in the early home, and how it can be transformed with creativity and maturity.

Most students of astrology begin with the study of their own chart, and continue to study their chart forever after, recognizing continued variations on the theme. Everyone has at least one significant fourth harmonic aspect in their chart. It seems to be a prerequisite for being born here on Earth. If there are moments in time when there is no tension among the planets, they are surely brief, and the obstetricians are out playing golf, and the pregnant moms are sleeping.

It is amazing how few words are needed to start thinking and talking about a feeling realm. When an astrologer does not use astrological jargon, clients get the point right away and need to be halted from telling you their whole life story. The aim here is to learn how to form congruent descriptions and to ask the right questions to adjust them, if needed.

There are countless examples that you may have already encountered in horoscopes from friends, family, and clients. We will concentrate in this book on the emotional processing of the hard aspects, and to pinpoint the emotions that live in the feeling realms. The house meanings are an essential part of it. Though there are hundreds of books that list the meaning of the houses, we want to refer to them in context of our feelings. Given below are the house meanings reframed as feelings.

- First house: self-image; how we feel about stepping out into the world

- Second house: self-worth; how we feel about embellishing our worth

- Third house: mental self-reliance; how we feel about communicating

- Fourth house: self-sheltering; how we feel about making roots for ourselves

- Fifth house: creating; how we feel about making creations

- Sixth house: self-help; how we feel about taking care of ourselves

- Seventh house: co-operating; how we feel about stepping out with others and being a partner

- Eighth house: co-owning; how we feel about combining our worth with the worth of others

- Ninth house: co-thinking; how we feel about thinking together with others

- Tenth house: co-inhabiting; how we feel about branching out in the world

- Eleventh house: co-creating; how we feel about making creations with others

- Twelfth house: co-healing; how we feel about taking care of the whole world

All of the houses are of course much more complex than that, but they nevertheless hold these simple concepts if we assign them that task. The first six houses are related to our primary development, and the second six houses are related to our immersion into the world, but all of it is self-development. Though the tenth house is the feeling of branching out into the world, and thus is our profession, like the fourth house, it has much to do with how we were parented, so of course we want to remain aware of the different ways in which we can experience our feelings about those houses.

When planets are in tension, the houses they rule are not usually in hard aspect with each other. They could be trine each other. It doesn't matter. The tension is by association. It works well with word pictures to first state the tension that is present between the planets and then move on to the affected houses. For instance, for someone with Pluto conjunction Venus, we might say: "There is a suggestion here that there is a creative tension between your need to get along with others, and your need to have deep control in the relationship." Then, if the houses that are ruled are the first and second, we could say "Your feelings about your self-worth are concerned with your feelings about self-image."

This was a real case of a woman with Venus ruling the Ascendant, and Pluto ruling her second house, with those planets in a square aspect. Her feelings about her self-worth were interfering with her feelings about stepping out in the world. This woman told me that she had never felt pretty in her whole life (though she was actually quite exotic looking). She said her father favored her pretty sister and she never got the same attention from him. He would more often than not turn away from her. In her teen years, trying to establish her self-worth, she let boys take advantage of her, which led to more self-worth problems, and then she resorted to manipulation to gain power over boys—and all because she didn't feel pretty.

This was a feeling realm that had a well-developed emotional dimension, full of troubling memories. It required a lot of emotional work to succeed in fulfilling this extraordinary Venus-Pluto need in a positive way. Now this woman is developing her power within herself and for others, instead of seeking power over others.

The emotional dimensions live within the feeling realms and are areas of memory. Emotions are *not* orderly, but as astrologers we categorize in order to bring sense to them. When stories come out, we want to be of help. When someone says, "Oh, but I feel so insecure," we look to the second house of self-worth or we notice that the Sun is square Saturn, for example. We are imposing an order on the emotions for analysis.

There are no good or bad horoscopes. There are only people who take less than perfect actions. All horoscopes have the promise of something wonderful in them, and the promise of something detrimental. Those who have become victims in early life, and it was not their fault, are survivors. If one becomes a victim later because of putting oneself in that position, then it is a lesson to be learned. We either make the effort to manifest what we want, or we let fate decide for us.

Every one of us on earth has a childhood in which we experience the taste of something painful, but no god inflicts punishment on little children. This is just life on earth. We come into circumstances on earth in order to participate in the energy that best fits our needs, although nothing really fits any of us perfectly because our real nature is to be divine. That is what we are here for, to become divine. We can do it slowly somewhere else in the spirit world or we can take the fast train here on earth.

Chapter 4

Emotional Dimensions and Emotional Memory

"There has been much tragedy in my life; at least half of it actually happened."—Mark Twain

We all know how it feels to experience sudden and spontaneous recall from a scent, a familiar face, or from a melody. Recall is linked to emotional investment in events and people, and the particulars of it are very personal to us. We find that people who have been together a long time sometimes have very different recollections of the same event, unless it is perhaps a very tragic one. Our emotional memories are so personal to us. However, collective experiences like the attacks on the Twin Towers in New York City are unifying events, not because we can agree on all of the details, but because we all felt the same impact.

There are people in this world—not very many of them—who can remember almost every little thing that has occurred in their life, and they can recall it chronologically and in great detail. Marilu Henner, an American actress, producer, and author, is someone who can do that. Marilu wrote *Total Memory Makeover* (2012), a book in which she talks about memory and what it can do for us. While she was being interviewed about her book, Henner said to journalist Dave Smith: "Memory is what makes life meaningful. It's that defense against meaninglessness. I'm not just occupying time. There's some significance to what I'm doing and how I'm living my life."

While the rest of us may wonder what sort of meaning can be gleaned from a bowl of Cheerios in the morning, people like Marilu with "hyperthymesia" make a point of storing the details of any given day. It is a way of ensuring that continuity will be retained throughout their life, and that nothing important has been missed. It is an act of faith that every day is or could be an important day, and maybe we just don't know it yet in the morning. We may not know it until one day when we look back on it, and see the significance of what came before.

Marilu says that the goal of her book is to lead people to a more conscious life and to encourage people to look for the "juice" in life, even in the smaller and more boring parts. One of the chapters in her book is on exercises that build sensory memory. If we have this kind of memory, Marilu says, then we will better understand where emotions come from, and we can allow ourselves to feel them without losing control. It also helps us to size up other people and to see for ourselves what is motivating them. In heated situations, she says, we will often overreact from a negative place. Having memories that we can refer to brings some perspective to the picture and allows us to slow down a too hasty reaction.

Some psychologists have suggested that hyperthymesia is only an extreme type of obsessive-compulsive trait, but Marilu and some other people with this ability disagreed with that on a *60 Minutes* episode in December 2010. They all believed that being able to remember almost everything allowed them to make connections between one event and another, and see the emotional connections. They actually took credit for developing their trait on their own.

When consulting with someone who is going through a difficult time in life, astrologers often see a significant outer planet

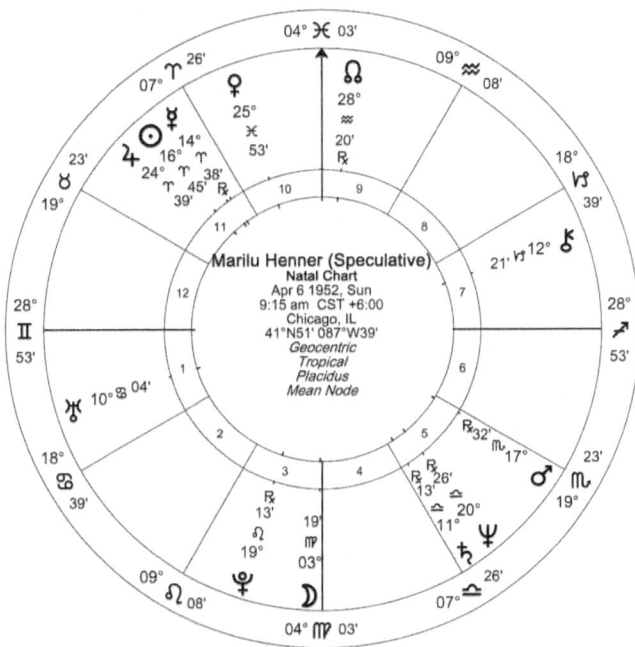

transit taking place and ask the client to try to recall what happened the last time that planet made a similar aspect. It is especially popular in the case of a Saturn transit for an astrologer to ask "What happened 30 years ago?"

Marilu Henner says if something happens that seems especially difficult or painful for her, she looks back in her rolodex of memories to find other emotional situations that resemble it. She is not looking for a particular date, although her events are also indexed by date; she is looking for a particular feeling or situation. She says she does this with intention, saying "What is the purpose of my fight with my brother in 1968, unless it is to inform the argument which I'm having with my son in 2011?" This is conscious soul development.

Marilu has a very prominent feeling realm in her chart that contains Mercury, so perhaps her need to create a special memory process for herself was extraordinary from birth. If we include

Emotional Dimensions of Astrology   75

the asteroid Chiron, there is a grand cross of tension in her chart that involves her thinking function. Mercury is challenged with an opposition from Saturn and Neptune and a square from Uranus, and lastly, on the other tip of the cross, is a square from Chiron. We could say that Marilu's need to think in a leadership capacity (Mercury in Aries) is in tension with her need to organize and give structure (Saturn) to the ethereal and the artistic (Neptune) while it is constantly being interrupted by the unpredictable (Uranus). It would be nice to know what houses are ruled but there is no accurate time available for her birth. With the Sun involved and opposing retrograde Saturn, we can guess that we should ask if the father figure seemed distant and not emotionally available to her.

Marilu's Mercury feeling realm was aspected by solar arc Venus at 10 Aries square Uranus exactly at 10 Cancer. That was in the fall of 1966 when she was age 14 and taught a dance class for the first time in her mother's dance school in their garage (from *Total Memory Recall*). Up until that time she was her mother's student. This must have felt like wings to her! Transiting Saturn was conjunct her natal Venus, so we know that it wasn't all fun and games at first—it was also very hard work. Venus, which rules her fifth house of creativity, made the solar arc to Uranus, and then to Saturn a year after that, and then to Mercury and the Sun, and finally to Neptune and Jupiter by opposition and conjunction.

This is what astrologers do for their clients. They look for the "big bells" and ask about life changes at those times. So what? Our lives do change. Marilu taught dance because she showed aptitude, and she earned the position. Ten years later, at age 24, when her film career started taking off, solar arc Venus was at 20 Aries, and opposed her natal Neptune. So what? We must ask our client about the emotions. We must somehow ask "What was going on emotionally? What did you learn from that feeling?"

Recognizing emotional dimensions and working with feelings is not about outwardly expressing emotion. It might be important to express ourselves, but everyone does that differently.

In another chapter we'll discuss the self-sufficiency of the grand trine, but please note here that Marilu's Venus in Pisces is in a wide water grand trine with Mars and Uranus. Her Scorpio Mars suggests her need to keep her actions controlled and private. The tendency of a water grand trine is to have emotional *expression* come out as efficient and tidy, but that doesn't mean that the emotions themselves are tidy. The trine allows ease of expression, not ease of inner work.

Since Marilu has such a powerful feeling realm with her Mercury, and such an extraordinary development of it, it seemed to me that finding another person who was born on the same date could reveal any resonance between them. The results were impressive.

Clayton Christiansen

Harvard business professor and financial writer Clayton Christensen, born in Salt Lake City on the same date as Marilu, has a different family background. Perhaps the Mercury realm is in houses of the horoscope which are business and finance related. His birth time is unavailable.

Clayton has been given many honors and awards for his creative theories on innovation in the corporate world, and he even coined the phrase "disruptive innovation" in one of his books. This certainly coincides with the importance of Uranus in the set. Like Marilu, he probably has Moon in Virgo because the precision and careful application in financial matters goes well with a Virgo Moon. While Marilu lines up her high-heel shoes (which she does with precision), Clayton balances data sheets on dollar return. Like her, he is fueled by his emotional dimensions.

Christiansen spoke on *Ted Talks* in 2013, where he compared a chart of how financial gain works in America to a chart of how self-worth is measured over a lifetime. It's an unusual topic for a financial expert, but he must have thought it was something he was qualified to do. First he presented a picture of how a capitalist enterprise will eventually topple—that we can only protect our enterprise for a while, after which it will be disrupted (Uranus) by other enterprising people. So we have to plan for this. It sounds simple, but Clayton is famous for his theories, so he must have a good point.

Personal development, Clayton continues to say in his *Ted Talks* speech, is not like financial development, because we are not competing with others. Our development is specific only to ourselves. Again, a simple thought but a profound one. He goes on to say that we are measured by individual moments in our life, and the important moments are times when we choose to build character. Notice he says that we "choose" to develop character—not that we just do it but that we chose it. He talks about the fact that when we die, we will be able to recall specific moments in our life when we had built character, and we will recall other moments when we were given the opportunity but didn't take it (he doesn't say why he knows this).

In an interview on You Tube, he was asked if it took courage for him to bring spiritual matters into his speech; he is not known as a philosopher or minister but as a financial professor and author. Clayton answered that it was his opinion that if we are afraid of doing something, then we should ask ourselves why we are scared, because that fear is telling us something. He said that if we are afraid we should look back into our history and remember another time when we were challenged like that in the past. Ah ha! Clayton was talking about the same thing that Marilu talks about! Both of them have developed these themes in their lives about using recall for emotional understanding! They both felt compelled to share that understanding!

Though not all of us will pay attention to every little thing that occurs in our life, we can, if we want to, think about events that

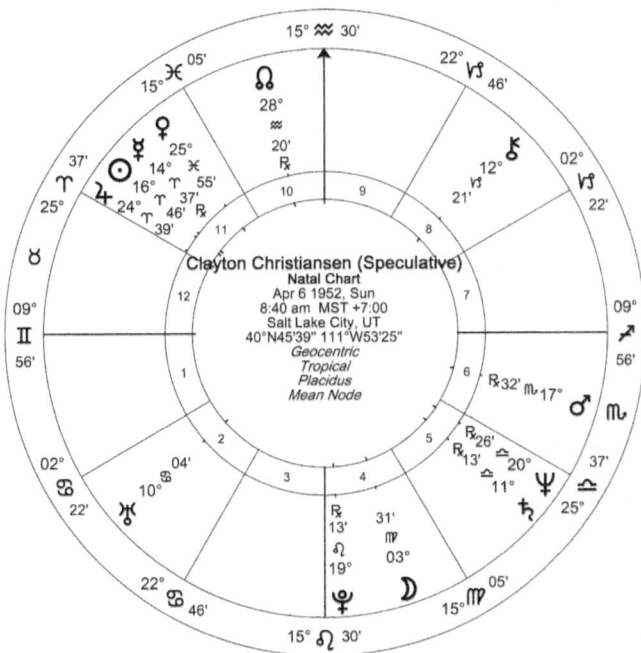

coincide with other events in our past. Astrologers can and do see coincidences like this with planetary movements that trigger the feeling realms. We can locate them with our software. Those are the moments Clayton was talking about. As long as we have these memories to refer to, we can go back and use them.

But it is not of course that simple. Before we can begin to look at some of our stored emotional memories, which are there for our reference, we need first to develop compassion for ourselves and for anyone who may have hurt us. Otherwise we are not going to want to look at those memories because they are sore points for us, full of sadness and regret.

Tenzin Gyatso, the current Dalai Lama, wrote in *Emotional Awareness* (2009) that the emotion of anger is natural and easy and dangerous; but compassion is not so natural and it must be learned through practice and discipline. Amazingly, he says that once compassion is learned it becomes part of our repertoire and, like any other emotion, accompanied by physiological changes in the body. That is, I am sure, quite satisfying to hear, since many people just assume that they do not have it in them to be compassionate.

This is fascinating to me because it suggests the possibility of true transformation. It proves the point that we are not just making academic adjustments to our behavior or practicing suppression when we work with our emotions. We are not pretending to live a certain way. If we can create compassion within ourselves through practice, then we can create joy or inner peace or dozens of other positive emotions that motivate our actions. Do we even know the extent of what those could feel like or what those feelings could produce?

The co-author of *Emotional Awareness* was psychologist Paul Ekman, whose field of study for years was recording facial expressions of emotions. One of Ekman's goals was to identify when people were lying. Appropriately, Ekman has Mercury opposition Neptune in his chart, so maybe, even when he was a child, he could tell when a person was lying; or maybe he was lied to many times and was tired of being fooled. Eckman took thousands of photos of people's facial expressions while they were lying. Wouldn't it be wonderful to record compassion on someone's face?

Although I've written here that working with our emotions in the feeling realms is a separate thing from expressing them, it is only half true because it is natural and healthy to express our emotions. Sometimes it is extremely subtle and it takes a very good reader to see them. Sometimes we feel bad all day because we are stuck in some unhappy place. Expression is about communication, and in reality we may not be able to transform emotions without interacting with others. However, we certainly need to do our own processing; no one else can do it for us.

American psychiatrist Judith Orloff, probably one of the few practicing psychiatrists in the United States today who does not routinely hand out prescription drugs for every little emotional blip on the behavior scale, says that what drove her to study emotional health was watching her mother's "ceaseless struggle to prove her worth" while she was growing up. Her mother was a doctor, and apparently it was extremely important for her mother to overcome all of the obstacles to what she perceived as a successful life. Judith writes in *Emotional Freedom* (2010), that she did not want to repeat her mother's emotional patterns in her own life.

Judith gave me her birth time. I won't publish her chart, but I know she has a Pisces Moon opposition Saturn in Virgo and square Mars in Gemini. That's a strong T-square feeling realm, and it is not difficult to relate that to how she saw her mother during her childhood. Without even bringing in the houses, we can say that the function of nurturing (Moon) is in tension with the function of getting things done (Mars) . . . in just the right way (Saturn).

Mars in Gemini is the need to accomplish action through both experimentation and precision, and Saturn is the need to structure the process with a very critical eye. There is every reason to think that the original tension that Judith experienced watching her mother can be transformed beautifully into an extraordinary form of nurturing, both for Judith and for her patients, but it takes an extraordinary amount of emotional awareness.

Generally speaking, many an astrologer would see Saturn opposition Moon in a chart and say that nurturing from the mother was cold and calculating. If this was true, it certainly might be because the mother was also required to take on the role of the father (for whatever reason) and it became too difficult a task. Mars adds to the impetus, suggesting that the mother was indeed busy (Gemini), and her big theme around the house was to hurry up and get things done (because Mom had to go to work). We only need to think about how that felt to a little girl.

First, every feeling realm feels like pressure, and children, especially, do not like pressure. It makes them feel as if they've done something wrong, when they haven't even figured out how to do anything right yet. As astrologers we have to know that is the whole reason why children experience feeling realms in negative way. Our parents are in the midst of their tense and often productive lives, and they don't realize that their children are only at step A. Children need to be given some credit for understanding, but they are still children.

Judith's book has a lot of varied stories about how transformation works. She recommends different modalities that might work for us, such as meditation, therapy, right eating, sleep and dreaming, etc. She has a chapter called "Uncovering the Spiritual," and she talks about living in service to the heart. She says that we cannot suppress our emotions, we can only transform them. Ha! It is the same thing I am saying!

Chapter 5

Three Moon Feeling Realms

"If you hear a voice within you which says you cannot paint, then by all means paint, and the voice will be silenced."—Vincent Van Gogh.

The Moon in the birth chart suggests one's percpeption of one's mother (or the dominant mother figure). It is not identical to how the mother truly was or how everyone else sees her. It is a picture of one's own experience of her. Precisely because of this, because of the familiarity of it as an example of caregiving, it is the way in which we nurture our self, hopefully with a positive version of it.

When we are young we run to our mothers for comfort, and when we are adults we look to our inner mother for that, which is the function of our Moon. If there is no hard aspect to the Moon, then the way we nurture ourselves is straightforward by sign and house. If there is a hard aspect to the Moon, finding comfort requires emotional work, just like any other feeling realm. Perhaps the Moon situation is a little different in males than in females, but largely we all need to nurture ourselves, and cannot expect a partner to provide us with it, just as we cannot expect a partner to provide us with the stand-up energy of the Sun. Below are some cases of Moon feeling realms that are mixed in with quite a bit of male energy. I call them adrenalin Moons.

Bear in mind that the Moon, accompanied by Mars or not, cannot take the place of the Sun energy, although it may appear to want to do that.

These examples are instructive in themselves, yet they are given here to show the process of discovering our feeling realms, regardless of what type of energy we are talking about. It is the awareness of these feeling realms which is the first step toward soul growth and the positive fulfillment of these extraordinary needs.

Angelina Jolie

A Moon in Aries is an adrenaline Moon, and a Moon in Aries conjunction Jupiter and Mars in Aries is a super-adrenalin Moon, a strong feeling realm. This is actress Angelina Jolie. Aside from her work as a model and actress, she is recognized for her role as mother of six children, noted for her nonstop work with charities, and for her bravery for publicly facing her risk of breast cancer. All of these things are Moon related.

Angelina no doubt perceived her mother as fiery, opinionated, and sometimes anxious and angry. Her father is actor John Voight, who left the family early in the marriage (when Angelina was only a year old) after he had some extramarital affairs. Her mother was an actress too, but she quit work after the divorce and dedicated herself to full time parenting at home. (Chart Data: AA Rating)

The fact that the mother took on the role of the father at the time is evidenced by Saturn in the twelfth house which is square to the Moon set. Voight was seldom around, according to Jolie, and Saturn in hard aspect with the Moon is very similar to Saturn with the Moon's node, suggesting that the mother was required to set the rules in the household without much help. Angelina's brother James also has Moon square Saturn.

---

[12] From "Blood, Sugar, Sex, Magic" by Heath Chris, *Rolling Stone*, July 5, 2001.

Angelina admits to having difficulties as a child. In grade school, she says, she was bullied for being too tall, too skinny, and for having big lips (sounds like jealousy to me!). In high school, rather than releasing her anger against others, she engaged in "cutting" activity, an obvious Mars in Aries type of solution.[12] She says she did it to make herself feel alive. At first glance we might expect that the Saturn in the twelfth house would tone things down for her, but it registered as a feeling of loss and disappointment of not having her father nearby and thus served to further fuel her anger.

We can try to paraphrase her feeling realm using the tools we've talked about here. Mars and Jupiter tightly surround the Moon. Starting with the functions involved, we could say that the need to nurture herself is in tension with the need to be assertive and to expand socially. In Aries, we sense the speed and impetuosity of it. The stellium is challenged by Saturn, which is the need to bring structure and reason into life, even from the twelfth house. In fact, since Saturn is almost exactly square Jupiter, which is a synodic cycle that indicates social reform in the world, we can say that Angelina would hopefully, as she ages, feel a strong need to effect social change.

Already a lot has been said, and we haven't even looked at the houses those planets rule. The Moon in the chart, the most important of the set, always equal to the Sun in its importance, rules Angelina's Ascendant. We can certainly say that her feelings about stepping out in the world (the Ascendant) were or are in very great tension with her feelings about branching out in the world (the Midheaven ruled by Mars). We could explore this in consultation with Angelina. We could ask her how upsetting was it as a child to avoid being seen and to contribute in expected ways in the world . . . and why?

The Saturn in her chart rules her seventh house, so we could say that her feelings about stepping forward into the world are also in tension with her feelings about walking with someone else in this world (seventh house). Did it feel to her like a personal attack as a child to know that her father disrespected her mother so much, that he abandoned her and his children? How will she transform her feelings of loss and abandonment and redirect her anger into something meaningful?

It was not until Angelina adopted her first child, she says, just prior to meeting Brad Pitt, that she knew she would finally be able to manage her own life, and, from an astrologer's viewpoint, build the strength which is promised in her lunar situation. As she took on the role of mother, she finally had something to do with all of that Aries energy. That Moon realm had been pressing on her for a long time.

Since we have knowledge of Angelina's early home situation, and because she has publicly voiced her dissatisfaction with her father,[13] we begin to understand some of the strong emotional currents in her life. After seeing the houses that are ruled, it becomes obvious how enriching it was for Angelina to go into acting, how suited it was for her as employment, as a way of working through her emotions. We should also wonder about the condition of her second house ruler, so that we can include in her consultation her feelings about her self-worth. What we see is the Sun ruling the second house in opposition to Neptune, which is another major feeling realm.

A Sun-Neptune opposition suggests that the need to stand up and be counted is in tension with the need to dissolve into the greater population. Again, like Moon in tension with Mars, these are two very different functions. Individuality is the opposite goal of collectivity. Many artists and actors and spiritually inclined people have this feeling realm in their chart, but it does not make it any easier to resolve. It is the working through the emotions which brings the dynamic to the surface, and then comes forward as art or prayer. In the meantime it can feel to a

---

[13]From "Jolie Also Splits from Dad Jon Voight" by Stephen Silverman; *People*, August 2, 2002.

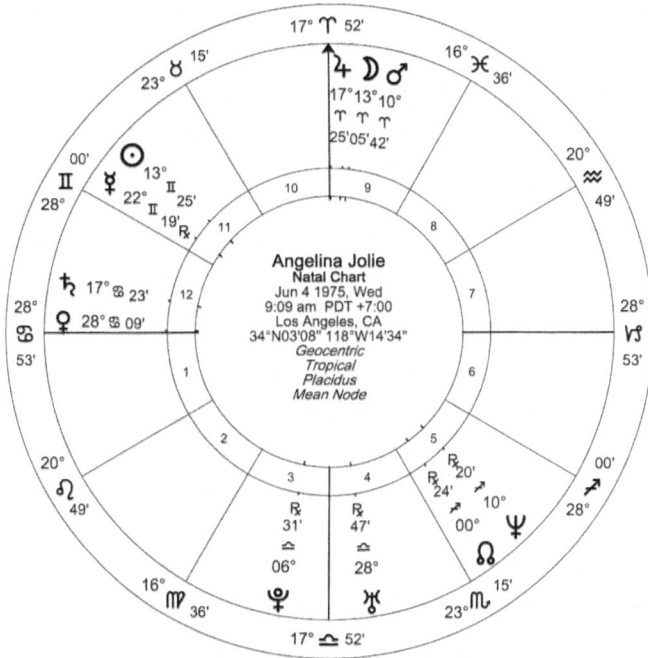

person as if they do not exist, even though they want very much to be noticed . . . a frightening and confusing feeling.

The ruling-houses picture of the Sun-Neptune enhances our understanding of it. For Angelina, the feelings about building self-worth (Sun ruling the second house) are in creative tension with the feelings about thinking with others (Neptune ruling the ninth house). This would have been something that was negative in her youth. But now she is known for talking with people all over the world and asking questions about their lives. She is drawing parallels between her own feelings and the feelings of people elsewhere in the world who have been traumatized.

If, after this type of analysis, as an astrologer, you have brought these suggestions forward to a client, and they profess to not recognize them as their own, it is a good approach to ask the person if they can recall a memory that coincides with some experience in that realm. For Angelina, we see an early trigger at age seven. Mars is seven degrees from a conjunction with the Jupiter-Saturn set. This is an easy solar arc measurement.

The summer that Angelina turned seven, her family (including her mother's boyfriend) moved from Los Angeles to a rural town in New York. This was a long way from home and from her father, though Angelina rarely saw Voight anyway. Mars rules the Midheaven, and the parenting dynamics had changed enormously because of the move. After noticing that solar arc, the next step is to look for transits that same year, and any pertinent Moon progressions, to find other confirming measurements. In Angelina's case, there are a lot of confirming measurements! We can be assured it would be easy for her to bring up emotional memories of that time. All we would have to do is to ask.

If we were in consultation with Angelina, we would look at the times later in her life that triggered that same feeling realm, suggesting to her that those times marked the same emotional dimension as the one at age seven, and ask her how her feelings have changed since then, and how she has developed emotionally. In 2011, when the Sun by solar arc was conjunct her Saturn, Angelina wrote, directed, and produced a film about a love story during the Bosnian war, *The Land of Blood and Honey*. Although the movie was not critically acclaimed, she was given credit for the difficulty of what she had done, for her accomplishment.

This was a major turning point in her life because up until then, although she had been involved in many non-profit organizations, Angelina had not produced any creative works of her own about her strong feelings on social issues. Her adrenalin Moon had, up until then, been fulfilled through her strong female character roles, such as Lara Croft in *Tomb raider* (2001, 2003), or the CIA agent in *Salt* (2010), which, though it released energy and supported the feminist ideal of self-sufficiency, was not a serious venture for her.

Angelina filmed another socially conscious documentary in Cambodia, which is based on *First They Killed my Father* (2006), written by a survivor of the Khmer Rouge regime. Transiting Pluto, ruler of Angelina's fifth house, had been making a square to her natal Jupiter and Midheaven. Normally, any Jupiter-Pluto hard aspect suggests pushing oneself to the limit. She pushed herself hard for this because it ties her Moon nurturing need to her contributions to the world.

It makes perfect sense that Angelina is particularly interested in children affected by trouble in the world. With her Aries stellium square Saturn in the twelfth, her Moon feeling realm consists of fighting against the disappearance of order, which always affects children. Children are in great need of being protected from these negative world experiences. Angelina remembers the disruption in her own home and wishes to transform her own pain as she helps others.

Amelia Earhart

Another woman who reflects a lot of pioneering spirit is America's missing adventuress in the sky: aviator Amelia Earhart. Her Moon, though not in Aries, was square Mars and Jupiter (so much like Angelina's!), with that similar adrenaline need. Her Moon was in Gemini, and, if it had no hard aspects to it, we could say that Amelia could nurture herself with things like reading and moving about, and trying many different things, all of which she did. But her Gemini Moon is in fourth harmonic aspect with at least four other planets, so it is a major feeling realm for her.

As a background to this, we see that Amelia had her nodal axis conjunction/opposition her Sun. So we could say that she could trust in life as long as she could shine in some way. The nodal axis is also square her Ascendant-Descendant, suggesting that she was required to be on stage as well, doubling that need to shine. Amelia's early years were spent in her mother's family home. Grandpa Otis was a successful federal judge and a respected man-about-town. He had a big house and a lot of influence.

Amelia's father was a failed lawyer and an alcoholic, although he managed to take some odd jobs in the town. He probably was an embarrassment to the family.

As a child Amelia could see that her mother held all the power in the immediate family, backed up the grandfather, and perhaps the whole town. I think there was not anything that Amelia did as a child that the whole town didn't know about. The lunar stellium in the second house in one way represents her mom, dad, grandpa Otis, and her grandmother, all crowded around her, with the Jupiter and Mars in the fifth house as her escape mechanism, her path to adventure! (Birth data: AA)

Amelia's need to nurture herself (Moon) is in a tense relationship with her need to have control in her relationships with others (Pluto and Venus). We notice that Pluto and Venus are ruling the seventh and the first house, bringing in the partner relationships which she saw around her: her parents and/or her grandparents. It probably appeared to her that someone always had more power over someone else, and that worried her.

We know from her biography that there were strained relations between her parents, and we assume that the grandfather had the final say because it was his home. A child would not want to pit her love for one parent against the other parent, or manipulate any power where love is concerned . . . but it probably occurred anyway. These are extremely complex feelings which probably carried guilt and frustration for a child.

The Jupiter-Mars conjunction is remarkable because it is so close; it is in the fifth house of creating some fun in life. According to biographies, Amelia's mother insisted on rearing Amelia and her sister as free spirits and to be modern girls. They were dressed in bloomers so that they could play outdoors like boys, and it was reported that Amelia's most favorite activity was sledding downhill in the winter as fast as she could.

The tension created between the two sets of planets in this complex feeling realm, the second house set and the fifth house

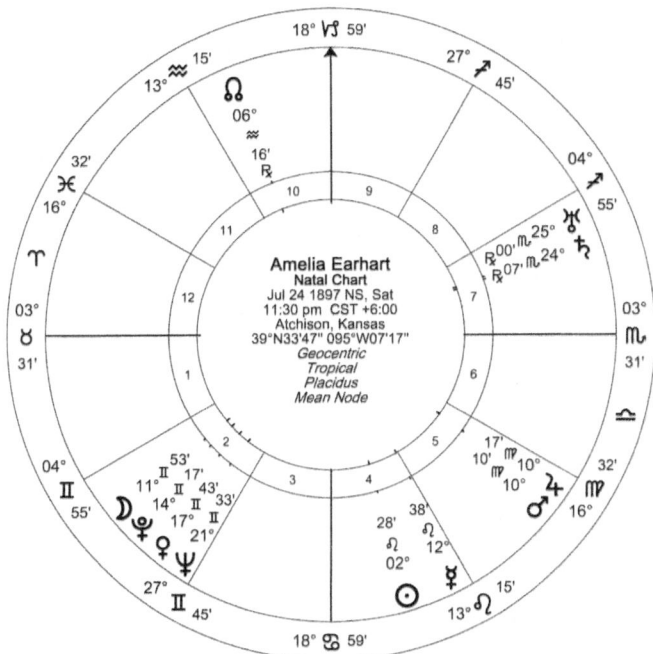

set, can be said to be about finding the right tools (Virgo implements), to enable Amelia to reach her true self-respect, her place of inner peace (Moon ruling the fourth house). Her household growing up was not peaceful, but it held her mother's faith in her (Sun-South Node in the fourth house), even if it was smothering her (Pluto next to Moon).

When Amelia was out in the sky, she was in her ultimate place, with less pressure around her, and literally less air. The Jupiter and Mars in Virgo, the need to take big action using precise methods, ruled the two most effaced houses in the zodiac: the eighth and the twelfth. Where was there to go? Her need to blend her own value with the dreams and values of others (the feeling of the eighth house) was in tension with her need to disappear into the void (the twelfth house). Although the sky can be mapped like any other place, ultimately Amelia "misplaced" herself.

Emotional Dimensions of Astrology

On July 2, 1937, when all contact was lost with Amelia's plane, her solar arc Sun was conjunct Mars and Jupiter in her fifth house. As in the case of Angelina Jolie's important solar arc Sun, Amelia's whole life energy was concentrated on the Moon feeling realm, the extraordinary need to exert extreme action to be able to find the place that nurtures.

Amelia was in the sky recording her actions when her end came. Accompanying her solar arc that year were the transiting lunar nodes arriving at her natal Pluto, ruler of her seventh house. Her partner was the sky itself. She was with "the other."

Her life is noted mostly for her mysterious end, and secondly for her contributions to the advancement of women's rights. In pursuing her extraordinary need for adventure, Amelia must have achieved some emotional growth and understanding along the way, as she patiently battled against the male prerogative to dominate all progress in the field of aeronautics.

Sarah Bernhardt

> "As for me, I am not placid. I am active, and always ready for a fight, and what I want I always want immediately. I don't have the gentle obstinacy peculiar to my mother. The blood begins to boil under my temples before I have time to control it."—*My Double Life*

French woman Sarah Bernhardt is said to be the most famous actress of her time (of all time, even). Her birth data is rated B, based on a consensus of two sources: her baptismal record, which also states the date of her birth, and Sarah's own belief that she was born on that day of October 23, 1944.

Her original birth certificate was lost in a fire. There wouldn't likely be any reason for Sarah to get her birth date wrong since her mother was alive and in contact with Sarah well into her adulthood. The birth time supplied by her brother has the Moon in tight conjunction in Aries with Uranus, with exact opposition to Mars. After knowing Sarah's history, we can only say that it

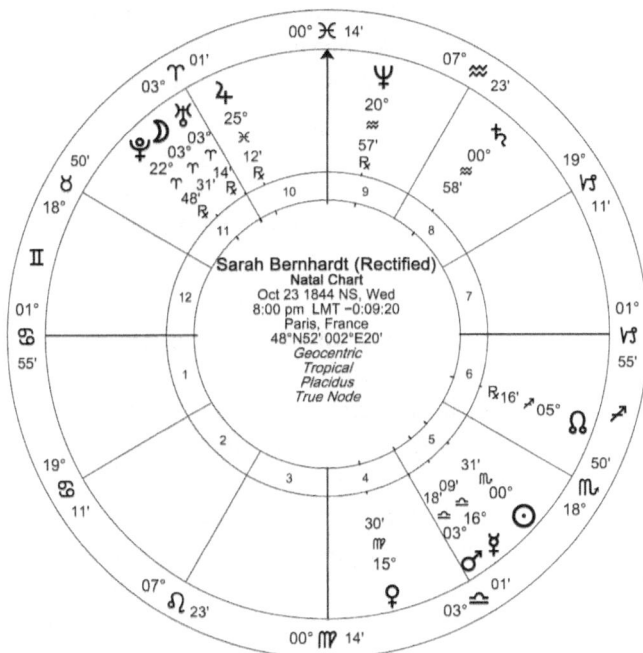

must be true. Her brother gave her birth time as 8:00 p.m.

Sarah had a lunar nodal axis in Gemini-Sagittarius, certainly suggesting that she could trust in life as long as she was communicating in a grand way. It was said that she had a uniquely clear and emotional voice, and her overly dramatic acting on stage was what people loved about her—that and her stage presence, her elegance, and her bearing.

Though it was a little early in history for Sarah to make a case for women's liberation, she was known to insist on personal liberation. Her mother was a high-end courtesan in Paris, and Sarah never knew her father, even if she did concoct a few stories about him. We could say that Sarah viewed her mother (the Moon picture) as fiery and unpredictable, but as per the quote above, perhaps she merely saw the strong independence of mind, or was just being facetious and her mother was just like Sarah.

Emotional Dimensions of Astrology

Sarah spent the first three years of her life in her mother's home in Paris, and then she was packed off to the country not far away to be reared in a small cottage by a governess. Her early history is sketchy. It surprised everyone later to learn that at age eight she did not yet have proper schooling, so she was sent to a Catholic convent for her education. Her mother was Catholic, despite her Jewish heritage and obvious deviant status as a high-class prostitute.

Sarah said she liked the convent, and she liked the mother superior there, who took her under her wing. She was known, however, to get into fights with the other girls, to lord it over them, and to have selfish tantrums. We see that when she turned eight in the fall of 1852, Jupiter was making a solar arc to the natal Uranus-Moon set at 3 Aries 15 and 3 Aries 31, respectively (per this rectification), and opposing Mars at 3 Libra 18. Boom, boom, and boom! Jupiter in general is expansion of any sort, so we know that her feeling realm was taking on dramatic proportions. Everything was blown up. At the time, transiting Pluto was making an exact opposition to her natal Sun which was at 0 Scorpio 32, and thus also square her natal Saturn, which was at 0 Aquarius 59.

This had to be an emotional time for her. Two feeling realms within her were being triggered at the same time: her Moon and her Sun. At such a young age she was taking stock of the realization that she had no father, and essentially, she had no mother either. Both Jupiter and Pluto, the activators, rule Sarah's sixth house, if this birth time is correct. The sixth house, among other things, is how we feel about taking care of ourselves, and how we feel about discipline. Sara did well in school, concentrating on taking part in school plays. She was learning how to be both father and mother to herself, quite a task for an eight year old.

We can say, like other Moon adrenalin people, that Sarah needed to nurture herself with excitement, and she had the need to be unique and make things happen. The Moon rules her Ascendant and also her second house of self-worth. We can say that Sarah's feelings about presenting herself, and her feelings about her value were challenged. She no doubt didn't feel good about who she was, in spite of her egotistical and selfish demonstrations. The ruler of the first house was in tension with the ruler of the tenth house. This suggests that gaining self-worth is linked with her worldly contribution and recognition. Allowing her roots to branch out in the world would be essential. Recognize the similarity between this and Angelina Jolie's Moon-Mars conjunction.

It's no shock that the daughter of a "kept woman" would be concerned that her fate would end up the same, and indeed, biographies suggest that it would have been a paved road for her since both her mother and her Aunt were well-known courtesans with social connections. Sarah had been introduced early in life (we don't know how early) to the art of proffering her wares, which, at that level of exchange, was not just physical and on the street, but intellectual, psychological, and artistic.

After age eight it was another ten years before another solar arc measurement arrived at her Moon feeling realm. Sarah was eighteen when solar arc Venus made a conjunction to her Mars at 3 Libra 18, again also triggering Uranus and the Moon. In the summer of 1862 at age eighteen, Sarah was accepted at the prestigious acting troupe/academy in Paris, the Comedie-Francaise. This was the best chance an actor could have hoped for! This certainly looked like a favorable solar arc to her feeling realm. It must have felt extraordinarily fortuitous to Sarah; but of course an astrologer might have warned her that accompanying this good fortune was the need to study her emotional dimensions as much as her lines, for this was a test to see if she was ready to apply her talent with compliance (Venus) rather than with so much defiance (Mars).

Barely eight months later, in early March 1863, before solar arc Venus had yet passed out of 3 Libra, transiting Neptune was at 3 Aries, and transiting Saturn was at 3 Libra as well! This was a critical time for Sarah. We see progressed Moon in March of that year square the Midheaven. Sarah foiled her best career chance, not permanently, but she couldn't have known that. She got into an argument with another actress, and slapped her. Because she would not apologize, she was fired, and she had to leave the theater.

So, our questions to Sarah at that time, because she undoubtedly would have blamed someone else for her misfortune, would be to ask her how her feelings could be connected to the time when she was age eight, when we know that those three planets were triggered by Jupiter. Perhaps we could get her to reflect on how her emotions had gotten the better of her. We would have asked her to focus on what those emotions were about and what she could work on within herself to believe in her worth.

Like many women with adrenalin Moons, Sarah just kept trucking along. In fact, she probably would not have given the time of day to an astrologer because she was always busy moving on to the next thing. Her failure at the Comedie-Francaise did not crush her after all, and she continued to bring attention to herself in theaters around Paris.

One year later, in March 1864, the whole Moon feeling realm made a solar arc to conjunct-oppose her natal Pluto. This looks monumental. A big slice of her emotional world (the slice that everyone saw on stage) was applying for a position of power. Was it a new job? Well, not quite.

Sarah just missed becoming the wife of a prince of Belgium. It would have been an impressive title for her, and a position of respect, but she wasn't suited to the life-style. She became pregnant with the prince's child in February. The prince was advised against marriage by his family, and there is no record of any financial exchange between the family and Sarah. It was Sarah's decision to have the child. Doing so sealed her reputation in Europe as scandalous, brave, independent, and otherwise the talk of the town. People flocked to see her performances. It was a good career move.

No one could say that Sarah Bernhardt did not succeed in life. She was an icon like no other. Those who were lucky enough to see her perform, even when she was age sixty-five or seventy, were impressed by her. It was said that there was no one like Bernhardt, though her acting today would probably be laughed off the stage. She was the world's first super-star. We cannot say if Sarah experienced any real soul growth in her life. Usually with people who do, there is evidence of a more lasting legacy for the world. But Sarah was singular and could not be duplicated. It was said that she was always generous and loving within her own family, particularly to her son, whom she spoiled all his life, and she did make tremendous sacrifices to establish a hospital for the wounded during the 1870 siege in Paris. We of course are not looking at her horoscope to judge her but only to see the opportunities in her life in which she could learn and grow. It was perhaps amazing enough that she survived her early life and became a star.

Chapter 6

Sun-Uranus Feeling Realm

How might a Sun-Uranus feeling realm differ from a Moon-Uranus feeling realm? What we need to remember is the difference in function between Sun and Moon. The Sun is concerned with outward manifestation, and the Moon with inward manifestation. Uranus, too, wants to move outward and make a difference. There is no nurturing involved with Uranus *per se*.

The higher expression of Uranus-Sun need not convey anxiety or excitement, although it is so often how we witness it, especially in comparison to other energies. There is also a persistent quality to it. Unlike being with the Moon, Uranus with the Sun is a good fit: like attracting like. Sun is about status, and Uranus is about unique status.

Finding one's guiding star in life can be painful, especially when it is a one-of-a-kind guiding star. It can bring the feeling of intense longing, and it can be a lonely quest. It's not so much about bigness, like Jupiter, although it can be associated with fame. It is never as easy as finding adventurous things to do because it usually has to be a very specific kind.

Martin Litton

Environmentalist Martin Litton, who did not achieve fame in his life, was a close friend of Edward Abbey, who was a well-known radical environmentalist in the 1960s. However, Martin did as much or more than Abbey to protect endangered wilderness in the U.S. Martin is often called an environmental warrior. His birth time is not publicly known, but rectification from his life's work and the date of his death suggests a Sagittarius Midheaven and a Pisces Ascendant. Placing his Aquarius Sun and Uranus in the twelfth house describes how much his status and work lived and thrived behind the scenes and in the wilderness. He was the leader of a few brave souls who could ride dory boats down the rapids of the Colorado River.

Since there is little history available of Martin's early life, and I didn't know him personally, I can at least acknowledge what I see in his chart, even without a documented birth time. We see that the lunar nodes are closest in aspect to Saturn (by six degrees) with an opposition to Mercury. Saturn is retrograde, echoing that the mother took over the task of enforcing the rules and giving direction. We can guess that Martin looked for concrete answers to questions, which is something that every Saturn-Mercury person does. This can be lifelong emotional work in itself, grappling with trusting the word of others, going over communication with a fine-toothed comb, and checking the facts with a discerning eye.

Early in his life Martin realized that the environment was his guiding star. At age eighteen he wrote a letter to a Los Angeles newspaper demanding that sensitive Mono Lake in California be protected. From that point on, Martin never failed to work to advance legislation to prevent land development that would destroy the natural environment. He fought successfully for the prevention of dams in several locations in the western U.S., most effectively with his words.

The agenda of Uranus, especially in its own sign in Aquarius, is to move forward without restriction. Martin's need to identify himself with unrestricted freedom in nature was linked by a circuitous route to his own personal comfort, represented by

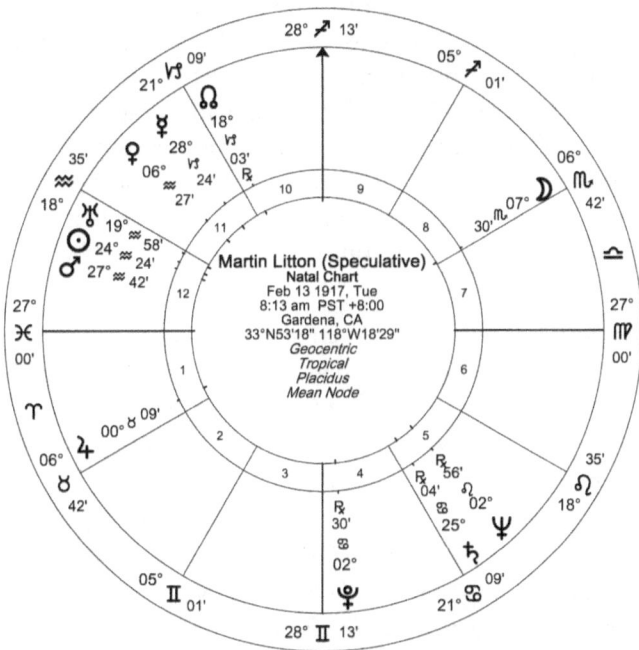

the Moon in his chart. The Moon was in Scorpio the whole day on which he was born, and so probably opposed by Jupiter in Taurus. His way of nurturing himself was to subject himself to the largeness of the wild elements in nature, to personally commune with their power.

We have to say that Martin worked daily with the emotional dimension of his Uranus-Sun-Mars conjunction. It was a feeling that he needed to fight for the land's right to manifest itself freely, at least without too much interference from humans. If he had not discovered his passion, he would have felt always that he was a stranger in a strange land.

On January 17, 2016, I saw the premier of a documentary about Martin called *Martin's Boat*. The creators of the film of course didn't know that on that day the North Node was at 23 Virgo 31 conjunction Jupiter at 23 Virgo 06, which opposed Martin's natal Chiron at 23 Pisces 59, close to the Ascendant

I chose. Transiting Mars on the premiere day was opposite the transiting Moon at 7 Scorpio-Taurus. My rectification of Martin's chart had already put his Moon at 7 Scorpio 30, and that was prior to my knowledge of what was happening in the sky on the night of the premier. My rectification may not be correct, but the relevance of the coincidence was not lost on me. Also, on January 17, transiting retrograde Mercury was less than two degrees from Martin's lunar nodal axis. The people at the premier fell in love with him.

The dory boat is a wooden craft that rides the rapids like no other craft. One needs to be highly skilled to do it successfully. The documentary showed footage of Martin steering his boat through treacherous and foamy waters, never once panicking or showing doubt.

The last time he navigated a dory was at age eighty-seven, when he was still a powerfully built man with the look and confidence of a sea captain. People were captivated and inspired by the film and the man. After the film had ended, one of Martin's friends said that when Martin died in 2014 at age ninety-seven, ten years after his last navigation, while reading the email from Martin's family announcing his death, an earthquake struck the house and knocked a globe of the earth to the floor. How perfect for a man with a Sun-Uranus-Mars feeling realm!

Jules Leotard

Another man who had the Sun conjunction Uranus and also conjunction Mars, this time in Pisces, was Jules Leotard, known as "the daring young man on the flying trapeze." He was the person who invented both the trapeze and the skimpy leotard that went with it—an outfit that allowed people to move with freedom. No doubt the skimpy leotard pleased all the women and maybe a few men as well.

Leotard's chart held a stellium in Pisces. Venus was there, with Jupiter in Virgo opposing, and Chiron making a T-square from

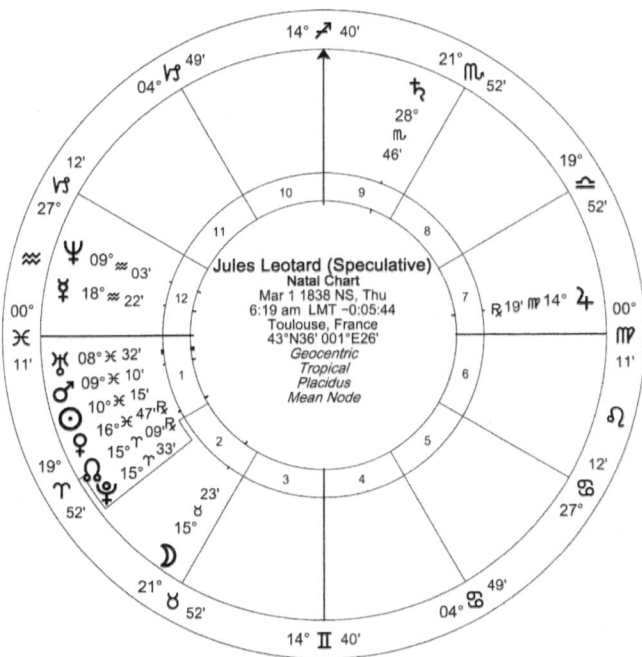

Gemini. That is a very loaded feeling realm all centered toward acquiring status and recognition in life. Pisces is the sign for artists and visionaries.

The beauty and glorification of the human body was just beginning to emerge at that time in history. Bodybuilding for men had become acceptable once again, lost since the time of the Roman gladiators and replaced with the modesty of Christianity. The man who was the father of modern day bodybuilding was Eugene Sandow, who had Sun very closely conjunction Neptune in Aries. He is accredited with the popularization of the concept that strong men are beautiful men, and they are entertaining to look at. Sandow was born thirty years after Leotard, and he looked much like Jules did in his tights. Jules was a unique pioneer of his day—so unique, in fact, that to some people he was another freak in the circus as he propelled himself through the air in his new leotard.

Emotional Dimensions of Astrology

Jules' father owned and operated a gym, and thus the father, too, must have been somewhat of a progressive. Astrotheme has a time of 6:00 a.m. for Jules' birth. If we adjust the time to 6:19 a.m., we see the solar arc Neptune (so graceful!) conjunction the Ascendant at 0 Pisces in November 1859 when Jules first presented his trapeze and demonstrated his art. We also see solar arc Uranus and Mars arriving at the Aries Point, a fine example of revealing a noteworthy invention.

When we look at the lunar nodes, Jules' trust situation in life, we see that the North Node is aligned with Pluto in Aries. His mother probably smothered him somehow, or insisted on fussing over him, perhaps giving him little space in his childhood for his daring. His Uranus and Mars are rising just before the Sun (oriental), and he probably drove his mother crazy with fear and worry that he might kill himself before he was out of her care. He needed to find a positive expression for his Pluto. With the trust profile in the first and seventh houses in Aries-Libra, we can say that Jules could trust in life as long as he could be the leader for transformations for his self-presentation and for the enjoyment of others.

Chiron at 16 Gemini square his Venus at 16 Pisces suggests there was a hurtful aspect to the whole thing. He was a performer and entertainer, and he would have wanted respect for his art. The stellium of planets surrounding his Ascendant suggests the need for protection of his ego, especially as they are so involved with his Sun. His invention of a swinging bar added movement and daring to a workout, but it also allowed the audience to see his body in fluid motion from below. To some, it was shocking and indecent. All of these things are tied in with the emotional dimensions which lived within him.

Having the Sun in hard aspect with Uranus as a feeling realm is about manifesting a unique status, but it is also about the feeling of the worthiness of the unique self. Our feelings regarding our status in life can, especially with the addition of Mars, take on a fight. Both of these men, Leotard and Litton, used inventions to propel movement through the elements in the world. For Litton, even though the dory boat had been around for quite a while, he customized and refined it in order to improve on the experience of riding the raging waters. His objective was to give others a better experience of nature. Leotard did something very similar. Both of them were dealing deeply with their Sun feeling realms.

Perhaps for men, more than for women, there is pressure to work so continuously with any Sun feeling realm, because status and ambition are still with us culturally. Men won't as often share their feelings about it, but they do experience them inwardly. Women, too, may work toward the development of their Sun expression, but there is not as much pressure yet for them to do so.

Chapter 7

Three Men and an Earthquake

On May 21, 1960, an earthquake struck near Santiago Chile at 6:02 a.m. as a pre-shock to an even more devastating quake the following day: a 9.5, the biggest quake ever recorded in history as of this writing. The quake on the 21st was an 8.1. That day, the start of a swarm that lasted through June, there was a grand trine between the Moon's North Node, Venus, and Saturn. I normally do not consider a grand trine as particularly wonderful or important (more on that in chapter 8), but in this case there is something to be said about it.

The Valdivia quake, as it was called, left more than 5,000 people dead and one million people homeless. In the days that followed, people struggled to find their loved ones and to help one another to survive the horrendous aftermath. Reflected in the astrology of the first jolt we see the Uranus on the IC, the disturbance of the land. People pulled together quickly to stabilize the situation and help those in need, and that was reflected in the grand trine of earth signs that included one end of the Moon's nodal axis. When a lunar node is involved in a mundane event, there is the propensity for the merging of groups of people for a special purpose.

That day, with Pluto square the Sun, even though that configuration so often manifests as loss of control and possible violence, people responded and pushed to control the situation. The North Node in Virgo was trine Venus in Taurus and trine Saturn in Capricorn. Nothing suggests organization like Saturn in Capricorn, and nothing suggests compliance for bringing comfort like Venus in Taurus.

The square between the Moon in Aries and Saturn suggests initiative, leadership, and organization as an extraordinary need, and it indeed would take extraordinary effort to secure any level of comfort and security. As a whole, the people of Valdivia seemed to bring their best efforts to a horrendous situation.

What would that same chart look like for a person who was born on that day? What are the feelings involved? The Sun-Pluto square would be a significant feeling realm for that person. A hard aspect between Pluto and Sun suggests the feeling of needing control over one's life, and the feeling of being overwhelmed by it. It can also be the feeling that there is deep strength within the self to deal with things that appear overwhelming.

Certainly many people were born on that day, maybe even some in Santiago. Three of them presented here are: political analyst Jeffrey Toobin, East Indian actor/producer Mohanlal, and serial killer Jeffrey Dahmer. This contrast/comparison is to show the vastly different circumstances that can accompany the same astrological patterns, starting with the circumstances in the early home. The tensions and the feelings are similar, but they were experienced on different levels and are about different things.

Of the three of them, we have learned the most about Jeffrey Dahmer through a book written by his father, and we can use that information here, with reservations. In interviews, Jeffrey's father is relaxed and open, and even suggests that perhaps Jeffrey inherited some troubling DNA from him, because he too has had some dark thoughts in the past. Jeffrey's mother, on the other hand, is a different story, and we shall get to her.

Jeffrey Toobin's parents were public figures, so a few things about his early home can be surmised from that. My last example, Mohanlal, has a less available early story, though we know that his mother was a stay-at-home mom, and we see her huggable round figure and her smile in photographs, and we know that Mohanlal learned to cook from her (he loves to cook) or at least learned to eat well from her. As astrologers we can make general statements using astrology, and apply it to what we know about a person's history.

Jeffrey Toobin

Jeffrey Toobin is a man who has appeared regularly on news shows in the U.S. He has received awards for writing and reporting, and for his legal analysis, and he has written six books. He had the distinction of being the first reporter to break the news about "pulling the race card" in the O.J. Simpson case, and he was the first reporter to interview Martha Stewart after the insider trading charges were made against her. Like his mother, who herself had an adrenalin Moon, Toobin feels the need to be first with his Aries Moon.

His birth time is not published, but we know some things about his mother that might help us with the Moon placement. In any case, throughout the day when he was born, the Moon was in Aries in a square relationship with Saturn, perhaps closer to Saturn than to Mars. I believe that he could have been born with a 23 Gemini Midheaven since he is in the communication business, and two important events in his career pinpoint that degree.

Toobin's mother was a remarkable woman who set a precedent for women in the field of journalism and reporting. Marlene Sanders worked her way up in the newsroom at a time in history when women were mostly secretaries, and often only instead of having children. She was a war correspondent in Vietnam, and was reportedly the first woman to achieve a nightly news anchor position on a major television network in the U.S.

Marlene's mother must have been formidable as well, judging

by the lunar node situation in Marlene's chart (b. Jan 10, 1931). Marlene had six planets in fourth harmonic aspect with the lunar nodes: Uranus, Jupiter, Pluto, Saturn, Sun, and probably the Moon! This suggests an influence from her mother to operate from a uniquely high powered executive position. We can surmise that Marlene lived with the feeling that she absolutely had to be in the middle of everything, within large social drama.

Because of her career, Marlene was away from home much of the time, and while she might have appeared as an exciting person to her son Jeffrey (his Moon in Aries), he grew to understand that her ambition came first; and thus, we can be assured of his signature of Moon square Saturn. This was both his impression of her and his own need to be nurtured by similar choices. He feels best when he is around fast action that is structured and supervised—and that is definitely a description of newsroom people.

If we look at the other two feeling realms in the chart, the Sun square Pluto, and the Mars square Jupiter, and the complex nature of the lunar nodes, we can begin to create a cohesive story around it—the feeling of needing to push for action, while slowing it down for control and structure, and also the feeling of wanting to be on stage (lunar nodes aspecting the Ascendant-Descendant) and wanting to contribute to the world (lunar nodes aspecting the Midheaven). It does not sound like an easy thing to do.

Jeffrey Toobin seems to have accepted his feeling realm of trust (lunar nodes) in the spirit of natural accomplishment because we see no deep underlying resentment manifesting in his life. At some point he may have appreciated how privileged he was, as he studied at a fine prep school and then attended Harvard. We could have said to Jeffrey Toobin in a consultation that he could trust in life as long as he could maintain his ambition (Saturn) and present his ideas on compliance (Venus) which would support his analysis (Virgo) of the group (a liberal one). If the

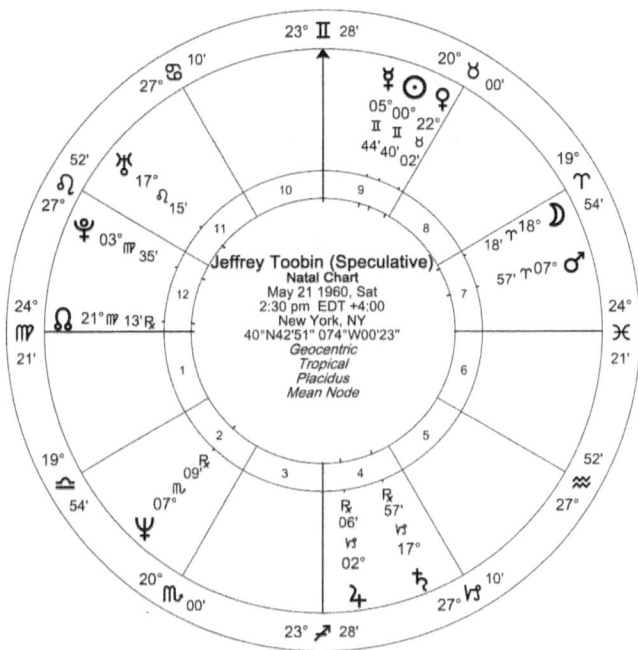

foundation makes sense, then everything else does, no matter how difficult the work.

However, in consultation, we would want to go deeper than that if Jeffrey was willing and able. When Jeffrey was age eleven in 1971, there was a solar arc of Venus making a square to natal Pluto, having passed the Sun three years prior. Here is the awakening of the Sun feeling realm, the deep feeling of needing control and power in his life. An astrologer would know to ask about that, as it is indeed part of his emotional dimension.

In 1971, when Toobin was eleven, his mother was hired for a news anchor position at ABC, a tremendous opportunity, and she continued to increase her status thereafter. Jeffrey had essentially lost his mother to television and the world. His father, perhaps, had never been around very much in the first place (Saturn retrograde). That year, transiting Saturn also made a square to Pluto. This was an extremely emotional time for Jeffrey

Emotional Dimensions of Astrology

regarding his identity and his worth. If we asked him to share a personal memory about that time, he would surely have one, and he could tell us exactly what it was, and how it felt to him and why. He would have remembered it well.

When Jeffrey was sixteen, there was a solar arc of Uranus conjunction Pluto in his chart, the second time in his life when he experienced extreme emotion surrounding his Sun feeling realm. If we could ask about it, he would tell us the details, and we can be assured that it reflected his need to create his own individuality in life, probably because both of his parents were so busy with their own careers that they had no time to involve themselves with his. This feeling of being singularly empowered (or perhaps singularly disempowered) was accompanied by a Jupiter transit conjunction to the Sun. With both Uranus and Jupiter involved, we know that the whole event was filled with some fanatical need to focus on his strength of character. Whether this event was foolhardy or disciplined we don't know, but it was emotionally meaningful to his future identity.

It is common for people who are politically ambitious to keep their emotions not only private but hidden even from themselves at times. A person with Gemini on an angle, which I think is what Jeffrey has, can even consider life to be two or more separate parts of themselves, one for the career, and one for the emotions.

Toobin had a lengthy extra-marital affair outside of his marriage which resulted in a child out of wedlock.[14] He takes full responsibility for the child, and he is still in a relationship with his wife and family, but these sorts of things are always messy. Perhaps he has learned something about his feelings and about his own soul growth through the emotional work that he has done. Perhaps he hasn't, and instead has little understanding of the importance of his emotional development.

---

[14]From "CNN Legal Eagle Jeffrey Toobin in Baby Mama Drama" by George Rush, *Daily News*, N.Y., Feburary 2, 2010.

In 2008, when Toobin's second partner became pregnant with his child and revealed that fact to him, solar arc Moon was square natal Pluto (rectification). This was the picture of two feeling realms coming together. It would have triggered old feelings and memories of not feeling nurtured when he was young. There is a situation of abandonment to consider, and not just his. When Toobin's baby was born, solar arc Sun was making an opposition to natal Saturn, bringing things full circle for him, with the understanding that he was repeating what his father had done by not being around to appreciate the life of his child. When the Sun and the Moon are both triggered, it goes to the core of ourselves. When two realms intersect this way, it is a protracted journey that requires, above all, a mature assessment of our feelings, and decisions about how we will change for the better.

There were also striking transits at that time. Toobin could not hide his feelings, even from himself, although he may have mistaken them for mere stress due to circumstances, and the fact that it would devastate his family. We have to assume that having an affair like that, for that long of time, might have been just an easy escape for him—a guilty pleasure to soothe harsh feelings that he never addressed well enough.

The grand trine in the chart holding Venus, could have allowed Toobin to think of an affair as just a temporary escape, a private way of feeling good for a while. But I don't think he got off that easy, not when so many other people were involved, including another child. He was forced into some very heavy emotional work.

Mohanlal

Mohanlal's horoscope may be somewhat less like the other two horoscopes because of the difference in time of his birth from the other two, where the Moon position was probably closer to Mars, and less tied up with Saturn. We have no birth time for him, except what I have surmised. There is much, however, that

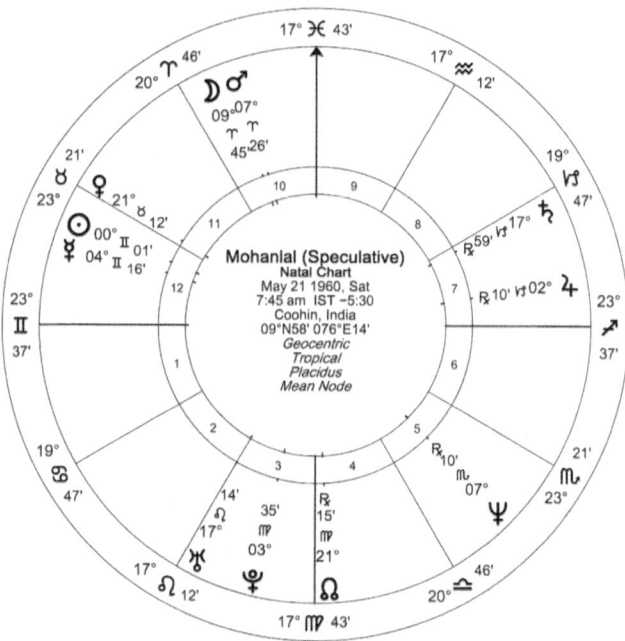

is similar, even without the time. The lunar node situation is the same, and the Moon, if it is part of the Mars-Jupiter feeling realm, is the awkward desire to somehow be the cartoon hero. Mohanlal, in fact, loves being his own stuntman in his action movies.

Mohanlal is an actor, director, producer, and sometimes a stuntman. He also heads many charities, and is a much celebrated person in India. He has been awarded an honorary doctorate degree from a University there, and he has received the 4th highest civilian award that can be awarded in India. His acting career began with villain roles and then branched out to include comedic roles and sensitive dramas.

It is unusual for any actor to play so many types of roles so successfully. If he was born around 7:45 a.m. with a 17 Pisces 43 Midheaven (which puts Neptune in his fifth house), the lunar nodal axis would touch all angles, suggesting his involvement with so many walks of life in India. An astrologer could say to him in consultation that he can trust in life as long as he can be on stage for the benefit of society.

We can surmise much by assuming the obvious, but we must be careful what we surmise if we have not spoken with that person. His success in life is not necessarily an indicator of soul growth. As an artist and actor, Mohanlal's life naturally reflects the work he has put into his emotional dimensions. Life is art, and art is life for an artist, but only if the person recognizes it that way.

Mohanlal said that he is very spiritual. He takes his life as it comes, artistically, spiritually, and as we can see in his dramas, emotionally. I would love to have him for a client. When he was age seventeen, when solar arc Uranus was arriving to conjunct his natal Pluto (something that occurred in the chart of every one of these three men), Mohanlal was working feverishly to become a wrestling champion, and also a playwright, an actor, and a film maker. At the same time, transiting Saturn was conjunct Pluto. When he was age eleven, as in the Toobin example above, when solar arc Venus made the square to Pluto, there was something of emotional importance, but I don't know what it was.

The comparison between these men has everything to do with the circumstances in their early home, which are the real clues to what the soul needs. By all accounts, Mohanlal loved his parents and his childhood does not seem to have been unusual; yet in consultation we might discover the roots of the tension that was derived from his early home. All of his actions seem to be productive and creative. If we asked his wife, she might tell us that he is impetuous and sometimes foolhardy (Moon with Mars), but our real question for him would be if he had experienced much personal growth in his life. I think it would be a resounding yes!

Jeffrey Dahmer

Luckily for astrologers, we do have the correct birth time of Jeffrey Dahmer. Though the story around Dahmer could fill a large book, most of us would not want to read it, filled as it would be with murder, dismemberment and the preservation of body parts. Jeffrey's father wrote a book about his son titled *A Father's Story* (1994), in which he tells us many things about Jeffrey's early life. We don't have to believe all of what he wrote, but there are reasons why Lionel Dahmer's story is more credible than the mother's direct refutation of it.

According to Lionel, Jeffrey's mother had an extremely difficult pregnancy with Jeffrey. She was said to have had seizures during her pregnancy that would stiffen her entire body and sometimes cause her to foam at the mouth. According to Lionel, Joyce was prescribed barbiturates by her doctor to remedy her seizures and her discomfort and fear. She denied that any of it was true, and said that her pregnancy was perfectly normal. If what Lionel said was true, many would say that the drugs caused Jeffrey to have brain damage. But Jeffrey was born, I think, more correctly with "soul damage."

In an interview with Stone Phillips on *Dateline* in 1994, the mother Joyce raved that no doctor would have ever prescribed barbiturates for a pregnant woman. She claimed that her husband lied, though she did not say why he would lie about such a thing, nor did she offer any statement from any doctor that barbiturates were never given. When we consider that the drug thalidomide was being handed out to pregnant women in 1960 to alleviate morning sickness, which ended up causing horrendous birth defects, the use of barbiturates doesn't sound so farfetched.

If we watch the interview closely between Stone Phillips, former co-anchor of *Dateline*, and Dahmer's parents, we see a father who is willing to take every responsibility he can for not seeing signs of disturbance in his son, and a mother who brought a lawyer with her to defend a position which she imagined she

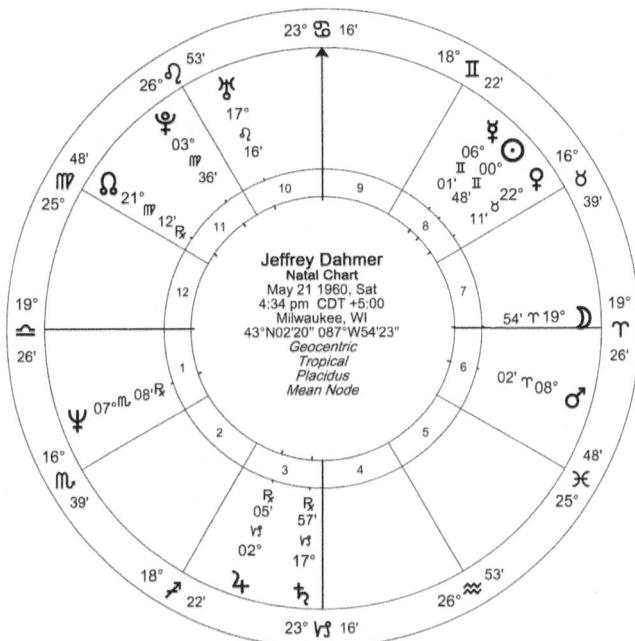

was in. She claimed throughout the interview that she had been misjudged all along by the public, and that everyone thinks she did something terribly wrong. She protested too much. Over and over she repeated that her son was just like any other son and that she was just like any other mother. She stated that she was writing a book that would explain everything about her husband and their marriage, but the book was never published. If it was that juicy, I wonder how she can think that her son was so normal.

In those early years, Jeffrey's father, like so many other men, was heading off to work every day or to university (studying chemistry). Joyce stayed at home with the baby, and by all accounts (Lionel's, Jeffrey's, the neighbor's) she was a materialistic and argumentative person, demanding better income from Lionel. During that time she attempted suicide at least once from an overdose of pills which she took for stress. She was said to spend much time in bed, recuperating from her numerous weaknesses.

Joyce (born February 7, 1936, Columbus Wisconsin) had Venus in Capricorn conjunction her North Node, which suggests her trust was linked to comfort and security, which is so often financially interpreted. Jeffrey said that there was so much tension and arguing between his parents that he would go outside and punch trees when he was a boy until his hands bled. Both parents were self-involved for one reason or another. If it was the mother's job to care for the son, and she was not able to do it, then the father was remiss for dismissing it as inconsequential.

As a young boy Jeffrey must have been expected to entertain himself and probably take care of his mother as well. Until he was age six there were no other siblings, so he spent all his time with a self-serving mother who felt sorry for herself, a mother who stayed in bed for much of the time. We might even suspect some form of sexual invasion of Jeffrey's space, if not outright sexual abuse. At age three, according to his father, Jeffrey had a double ingiunal hernia which required surgery, and it prompted Jeffrey to ask his mother if his penis would be cut off in the operation. Something like that is not an entirely ridiculous fear for an imaginative child, but all things considered, it is at least suspicious. This was when solar arc Sun was exact to Pluto, and solar arc Pluto was exact to Mercury. In Jeffrey's case, Mercury rules the twelfth house of critical illness.

At age four and a half, Saturn made a solar arc to 22 Capricorn, forming the exact trine within the grand trine of the lunar node. This, along with transits at the time, suggests something quite sticky with the mother. Transiting Jupiter was conjunct natal Venus, while transiting Venus was making a square to the natal lunar nodes. This repetition of Venus in the horoscope is striking. In addition, transiting Saturn was making an opposition to natal Pluto, suggesting some difficult emotional event making demands on the self-worth (Pluto rules the second house).

Why does one horoscope manifest in these ways and not the

other two? The answer is because these are different households and different souls, and the different birth times prove it. Mohanlal and Toobin probably had their own annoyances with their mothers, but Dahmer's mother was on the verge of psychosis, if not fully psychotic.

It was at age four when, according to his father, Jeffrey was first drawn to the bones of dead animals they'd found under the house. He was fascinated with the sound they made when they were rattled inside a container. A poetic resonance of that is reflected in the position of Saturn, the ruler of bones, arriving by solar arc at the fourth house cusp (the home) in his chart. The mother Joyce said she doesn't remember anything about bones under the house. Certainly in hindsight it all sounds a little creepy, but bones do make a good percussion instrument. It wasn't really all that weird . . . not at first.

When Jeffrey's parents visited him in prison, so many years later, during the Stone Phillips interview, we see Jeffrey embracing his father but ignoring his mother as she deliberately stepped away from him. It is an odd thing to see because it is usually the mother who exhibits unconditional love for her children, regardless of what monstrous thing they have done. A mother would prefer to think that her son is brain damaged than to think that his soul has wandered so far into cruelty and evil that she cannot comprehend it. Maybe she did comprehend it. Maybe she succumbed to evil herself. Why else would she not admit to taking barbiturates which might have caused damage to her son's development?

Never in Lionel's book or in the interview does Lionel blame Joyce for the unspeakable crimes their son committed. In fact, Lionel writes that perhaps Jeffrey's early interest in taxidermy, something that Lionel encouraged, was accidentally imprinted on his sexual coding, or that Jeffrey had gleaned dark energy from Lionel's own dark side without anybody realizing it. Such was Lionel's earnest search for answers and his feelings of guilt and failure as a father. It was at age eleven that Jeffrey, with help from his father, learned how to clean bones with chemicals and store body parts of animals. Lionel merely thought of this as scientific interest, since he himself was a chemist and had a scientific mind.

As seen with Jeffrey Toobin, eleven years of age saw the solar arc of Venus and the transit of Saturn square Pluto. Whereas this was awareness for Toobin that his mother no longer had time for him, and it was his realization she would remain forever more interested in her cold ambition than in him, for Dahmer it was something far worse. An "icky" relationship with his mother was replaced with darker thoughts on the nature of death. Death was attractive to him; such was the depth of emotional pain which he suffered. It would be difficult at this point in his life, though not impossible, for someone to talk with him about what was going on with his memories, and what new memories he was creating then. Imagine someone, not even an astrologer, but someone who cared, talking with Jeffrey at this age.

By the time Dahmer was age sixteen, when solar arc Uranus was conjunct Pluto, while Monlahal in India was working hard on his creative enterprises, Dahmer was just trying to hold on to any sense of normal. He was getting drunk all the time and avoiding any contact with his parents, who were in the middle of a divorce, who were certainly not paying any attention to him. He later told about his strong desire at this age to bludgeon to death a particular young man and how he laid in wait in the bushes with a baseball bat for his prey. He waited one year until 1978, when transiting Mars was conjunct to Pluto, and he let himself execute his first kill. And we know the rest.

In November 1994, Dahmer was killed by a prison inmate who had natal Pluto exactly conjunct Dahmer's North Node. In Dahmer's chart at the time, solar arc Moon was conjunct his Venus at 22 Taurus. There's that 22 Taurus again! It was said that he intimidated the fellow inmate, knowing that it would mean certain death for him. He obviously wanted to die. He had never been able to nurture himself normally (the Moon), nor to accept that his trust in life could be normal (lunar node), nor to get past the most rudimentary reaction to his frustration over lack of control (Sun-Pluto). He opened himself instead to complete darkness.

Dahmer had a disturbing childhood, but other than the conjecture that his mother might have sexually abused him, he perhaps had a childhood that was no worse than many. Perhaps his life was the latest succession of many downwardly spiraling lives that he lived. He was ruled by the courts to be sane. When he was caught, the authorities found a Satanic altar in his basement, and discovered a throne on which Jeffrey sat. He said it made him feel good.

There is always a possible darker version of ourselves while we are on Earth. While the earth signs tend to focus on security and material understanding and value in life, there are worthy manifestations of that. Dahmer's fascination with the bones of animals, and even the mechanics of human death, could have been a respectable and meaningful vocation. Lionel was right to wonder if he could have done more for his son. But in the end, Jeffrey probably only had himself to blame.

Chapter 8

The Idealism Feeling Realm

"There is no should or should not when it comes to having feelings. They're part of who we are and their origins are beyond our control. When we believe that, we may find it easier to make constructive choices about what to do with those feelings." — Mr. Rogers

This chapter focuses on the profiles and discussions of two men who were born a few years apart. They both had a connection with children, although one of them did not think he had that connection. When you put their horoscopes together you can see the zodiacal points where they connect, although I doubt if they ever met each other. One of them consciously worked at presenting his idealism as a goal, and cultivated harmony within himself, and the other brooded over life's incongruities, and responded to grief with comical drawings of loneliness and despair. I put the two men together in this book because they are two of my favorite celebrities, and, as different as they are, they somehow are neighbors. They both have great idealism, with a Mercury-Venus conjunction in Pisces, which has a natural tendency to dream of la-la land.

Fred Rogers

Fred Rogers was exactly as he was portrayed on his television show, *Mr. Rogers Neighborhood*. He preached kindness and compassion, teaching children how to have respect for themselves and for others. He walked around the make-believe neighborhood he created on his set and had conversations with the puppets, demonstrating how to listen and to how to respond to life's dramas. The show was a perfect expression of Fred's horoscope (Chart Data: Rating A). If the planetary dots were connected in his chart like in a child's coloring book, it would resemble nothing so much as a kite flying happily in the air, with a couple of loose ribbons floating around. That is not to undermine the seriousness of astrology, or the importance of Fred's life, but to draw attention to the joy that came through in his life and his television show.

The lunar nodes in Fred's horoscope suggest that Mr. Rogers could trust in life as long as he could share his art to inspire self-worth. The lunar nodes are on the edge of the second and eighth houses, the houses of self-appreciation and respect for the worth of others. One of the famous lines from Fred's show was: "I like you just the way you are." He repeatedly told his young audience while looking into the camera as if he were speaking directly to each child, that there is "no one else like you." He taught that each of us deserves to have special recognition. Is it any wonder that the lunar nodes in his chart are square to the Moon in Pisces, ruling the third house of communication and story-telling? It was his life's mission to translate harmony, and in that way he trusted in life.

Not much is known about Fred Rogers' childhood. A mother and father were present in the home, as was Fred's maternal grandfather, whose last name was McFeely. Since Fred used the name McFeely for the much-loved "speedy-delivery" postman on his show, we can assume that he loved his grandfather very much. It is documented that both his mother and his grandfather were musical, and they spent time with Fred as a child singing and playing the piano with him. Since Saturn is also involved in the lunar node picture, we know that the mother had to take on some of the father's role, probably with the help of the

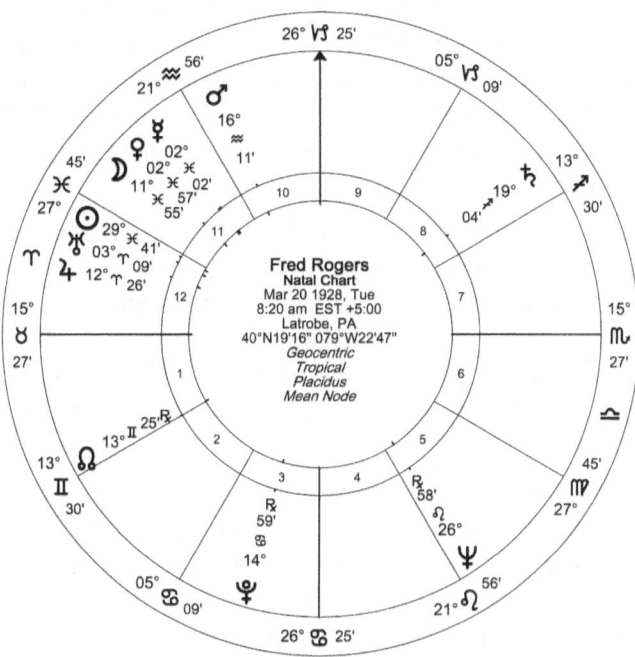

grandfather, as a secondary role model. Except for the father's name, nothing else has been reported about Fred's actual father.

As a foundation of trust, the lunar node situation in Fred's chart went a long way in supporting the rest of his chart. The Moon itself ensured that public contact and concern would be paramount in the life, especially since it is in the eleventh house of social endeavors, and again especially because it is oriental to the Sun, rising just prior to it, a measurement that is very common for a guru or teacher in the world. Saturn in Sagittarius echoes this ministerial position and, indeed, Fred was an actual minister. But what is the foundation of trust supporting in the chart? What other fourth harmonic feeling realms are holding and supplying the energy for his creative life?

Aside from the fourth harmonic aspect, which is involved in the lunar node situation, Fred had Jupiter square Pluto, Uranus conjunction his Sun, and Mercury conjunction Venus, a clas-

Emotional Dimensions of Astrology 125

sic formation of idealism within the very close conjunction in Pisces. Astrologer Noel Tyl has maintained that whichever house in the chart holds the idealism of a Mercury-Venus conjunction, therein lies a person's grief. In Fred's chart, Mercury and Venus are in his eleventh house, the house of the expanded neighborhood, the larger community.

Mr. Rogers' theme song was "It's a Beautiful Day in the Neighborhood," and we know that he longed for neighborhoods of people (and more) to be harmonious and beautiful. His Mercury-Venus is a very strong feeling realm. His grief was for the non-realization of peace in this world, the failure of people to get along, find possibilities to compromise and adjust to another person's needs.

Fred was always a bit distinct from others, but not especially odd, nothing more than quietly unordinary. The Uranus-Sun conjunction in the twelfth house is not anxious to emerge into the business of the day; it instead lives in the feeling of singularity, of being the special case, and going it alone.

Wavering between trepidation and pride might have been overpowering as a child. As he grew up, perhaps around age twelve when Jupiter made its return, he would have become more aware of his strength to move forward and outward, adding memories to his feeling realm of Jupiter square Pluto in the third house. He must have discovered that the words he uttered had power to them. He would have started working through those emotional dimensions or else be stuck in grief, loneliness, and anger.

When someone delves into the feeling realms and then works through them successfully, it shows up in their personal and professional lives. It even shows up in their handwriting. Author Tim Madigan wrote a book about his friendship with Fred Rogers (*I'm Proud of You*, 2007) in which he publishes a handwritten letter from Fred telling him how proud he is of his friend. We see distinctive writing, to say the least.

Every small case letter "f" on the page of the letter is drawn as a big bubble in the upper loop, and it makes the page look as if it is full of balloons! It looks like a fairground of people walking with their big dreams. There are also larger than average spaces between the words, which normally in handwriting analysis will suggest a person who needs space between themselves and other people. Fred's conjunction of Uranus and the Sun, notably at the Aries point, is a picture of a person who not only requires space between others, but time alone behind the scenes. Fred also allowed the space for others to be the individuals they are.

On July 9, 2002, when Mr. Rogers was given the Presidential Medal of Freedom for his work with children, there was a solar arc of the Sun to the lunar nodal axis in his horoscope. His Sun was shining not on himself but on the relationship he built with his audience. At the time he said, "Maybe they'll tell me one day why I got this award." One year later, when he passed away, there was a solar arc of Saturn conjunction his Venus-Mercury pair in Pisces. It was a natural ending for all the time he had spent transforming his grief into compassion. It pointed to the position of authority he had acquired as teacher and minister.

Edward Gorey

Edward Gorey was an illustrator/designer for the theater of the bizarre and the macabre. He was an odd person, an eccentric, and he located the odd image in his brain and then assembled it into a story through illustration. You may not have heard of him, but you've probably seen his work. His work is strange and funny. You can read about his life best in *The Strange Case of Edward Gorey* (2011).

During his lifetime he lived in New York City and later in Cape Cod, and was known in both places as a recluse, though not entirely. He was a person of dichotomies and anomalies. He had many artist friends, and he procured a standing invitation to rehearsals at the New York ballet, where he could be seen every day. He would not go at night for dislike of the crowds.

Children were largely featured in his drawings, yet he was known to be indifferent to children, and when asked one time what he thought of them, he said that he didn't know any, so he couldn't really say. He had been an only child in his home, and he admitted to being a lonely one. He said that growing up he would read the books his parents read, Agatha Christie novels and other murder mysteries. Though his illustrations rarely if ever showed any blood, and most were in black and white, there was danger always lurking around every corner in them. People said he was "gory" but that was really just a bad pun on his name.

He was not gory. We know that Edward was morose. He collected Victorian postcards of dead babies in their coffins, which was a common format in that era for letting friends and family know that the baby had died. He claimed that he was merely attracted to a postcard one day at the flea market, and thereafter expanded his collection whenever he came across them. He collected many other things, too, and surrounded himself with small treasures of all sorts.

His illustrations resonate with his lunar node situation; particularly with Saturn in Scorpio. In Edward's birth chart, the lunar nodes are in a grand square of energies, in a close square with Saturn in opposition to Mars. They are widely aligned with the Neptune-Venus opposition. Should we ever look at a complex lunar node situation and say that someone might be born with mistrust in life? No. Some people have problems with trust, yes, but the lunar nodes describe the conditions required for trust. These conditions will be present in one way or another, and require positive expression of them.

Gorey was a contented person, mildly friendly, and wanted nothing more than to practice his art. He never had a romantic relationship with any one person, and he claimed that it didn't bother him, that he didn't miss it. He may have been asexual, and he said so himself. Although he loved the sight of a ballerina stretching, it was a purely artistic interest. Or so he said.

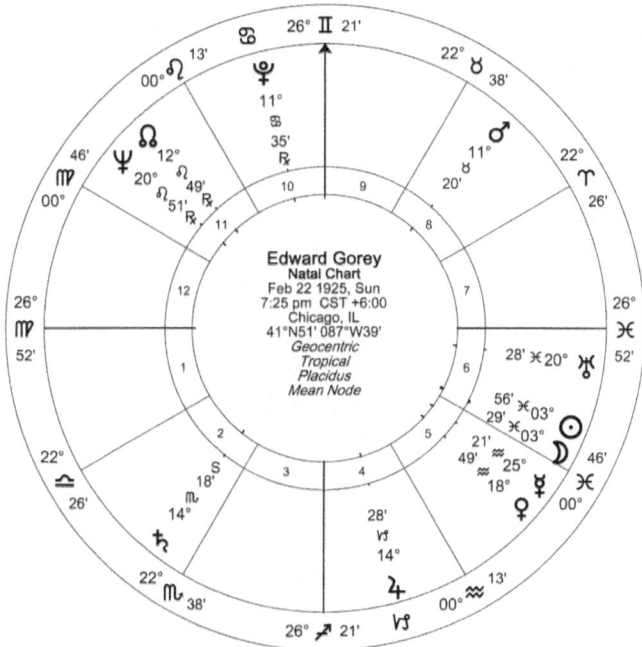

Neptune, ruler of Edward's seventh house, was lodged within that grand square, as was his Venus and Mars (Data Rating: AA). He enjoyed a very private world of his creations, collections, and pet cats, and it would have been difficult for anyone to intrude on that. Does that mean that he had a problem with relating to another person? Traditionally, yes, but also traditionally, anyone who is fully devoted to their craft or profession has little time or interest for a relationship with a person, and the art becomes the partner.

Without connecting with Gorey himself we cannot know what circumstances in his early home exactly reflected his lunar nodal picture, but we know that it related to his mother. If his mother was mysterious and aloof (Neptune opposition Venus in Aquarius), she was also the strict enforcer of the rules in the household (retrograde Saturn with the nodes), taking over the role of father.

Gorey's parents divorced when he was eleven, although if we look at the astrology it suggests it was age twelve. At that time, we see solar arc Neptune opposing the Sun-Moon pair which is at 3 Pisces, and this is where we see so much idealism in him, echoed by the Mercury and Venus pair in Aquarius. We could have asked Gorey in consultation what his hope had been for the relationship between his parents when he was young, and if he avoided seeing their real relationship in favor of some happier version.

If the father was actively present in his life, we would see it in the horoscope, but the Sun is almost consumed by the Moon. In fact, the Moon blocked out the Sun in the early degrees of Aquarius one month prior to Gorey's birth, and the eclipse was visible from Gorey's hometown of Chicago. The morning of his birth, the Moon was in Aquarius once again, and it came up over the horizon just prior to the Sun that day. We have to assume that the father was the weaker personage of the two parents.

Years after the divorce, the parents reunited (probably at the mother's bequest); in between, the father was gobbled up by an exotic cabaret singer. There must have been something quite appealing about the father, although strength of character probably was not it.

There was something sinister in Gorey's early home. One odd book he wrote, *The Beastly Baby* (1995), was about a teddy bear that strangled babies while the parents socialized and played cards in the other room, oblivious of the goings on in the baby's bedroom. The book has an illustration that shows the back of a strong looking woman at a card table, facing away from the child's room while she holds her cards. Does this portray Gorey's childhood, living silently in an adult world, overstimulated by his own imagination?

If we were to make a statement for Edward's feeling realm of trust, it could easily become too complex, so we would need to pare it down. Since the lunar nodal axis is in the eleventh and fifth houses, most importantly we need to say it includes the need for creativity. Neptune and Venus concur and amplify that. However, Saturn and Mars are big, thick, metal monkeys, or monkey wrenches, which might turn that dream into a nightmare.

The most acclaim that Gorey received as an artist, aside from his growing number of secret fans, was in 1977 when he received a Tony Award for best costume and set design for a Broadway remake of Dracula. On October 20, 1977, when the play opened, solar arc Pluto opposed his Sun-Moon at 3 Virgo. This was the same emotional dimension triggered by Neptune solar arc at age twelve. Also on opening night, transiting Uranus at 11 Scorpio 11 was opposed to his Mars at 11 Taurus 20. Amazingly, in 1937, when Edward was twelve, during the solar arc of Neptune, the transit of Uranus was conjunct Mars at 11 Taurus 20 on May 31 of that year. Did Edward realize that the emotional memories he held from age twelve were being re-triggered in 1977, with new and better memories? I hope so!

Obviously it was a happy night for him. It was more than a happy night. Gorey must have realized that his yin and yang (his Sun and Moon) were now mended and powerful, not broken and hurting, as at age twelve. The grief that resides in his fifth house, which probably would always be there just a little bit in life, was healed by the act of creating. That is how we do it, it's how it's done. As an adult, Gorey achieved what was so impossible to achieve when he was growing up. (Chart Data: AA Rating)

Chapter 9

Feeling Realms and the Grand Trine

"Nothing in the world is worth having or worth doing unless it means effort, pain, difficulty...I have never in my life envied a human being who led an easy life. I have envied a great many people who led difficult lives and led them well."—Theodore Roosevelt

Western astrology has sung the praises of trines since the advent of the psychological approach at the turn of the 20th century. Everybody who knows a little about astrology seems to want trines in their chart because they have been told that trines make our lives easier, and they represent our talents, the ones we have already "earned" in our past lives with hard work. I think the truth is far more complex than that, just as it is also too simple to say that if we are suffering in this lifetime, then we have been the cause of suffering in another lifetime.

I believe that trines are rather a slippery slope, and they can be lessons in themselves. Ease is not always beneficial, because human tendency is to depend on it for escape or for getting attention from others or just for being lazy. Besides that, various detrimental events can occur when trines allow for an easy release, when there is nothing else to provide caution.

The concept of having three planets linked closely by element is considered a loop of self-sufficiency. The motto becomes, "I can do it myself." Two-year-olds say that when they want to assert their autonomy. Whatever the expression is by element—earth, air, fire, or water—that is the way grand trine people keep themselves above the crowd. It always feels good to be proficient, but ultimately, it is a lonely position, and it can be a trap. If we consider the fourth harmonic aspects to be our primary treasure in life, then the trine aspects can only serve as helpers. It is when we use the trines as escapes that we get into trouble.

In the past, astrologers would look at a hard aspect of planets, and say, "Oh, but look! The trine is the way out!" Then they would discuss what great talents should be exploited to "get over" the bad situation, or around it; in other words, to avoid it. And that is exactly what a grand trine person will do, is to move straight into the trines, and avoid the messy feeling realms. It's like skipping a nutritious meal, to go directly to the chocolate cake, which just turns out to be fattening and makes us weak.

Stephen Hawking

One of the most striking examples of a present-day grand trine is that of scientist Stephen Hawking. It holds his Mercury! Stephen has a grand trine in earth signs, which, by element, implies practicality and material self-sufficiency. It seems quite incongruent that he has the earth grand trine, considering how dependent on others for physical care he has become. However, if we let the grand trine refer to his self-sufficiency within mental constructs, then it all makes sense. His thinking is geared to explain the known universe, all by himself.

In Hawking's chart, Mercury in Capricorn (the most hardcore, realist sign in the zodiac) is in a trine with Neptune in Virgo, and in a trine with Saturn and Uranus in Taurus. Saturn and Uranus are the two planets most often associated with scientific work. Neptune might be the planet most often associated

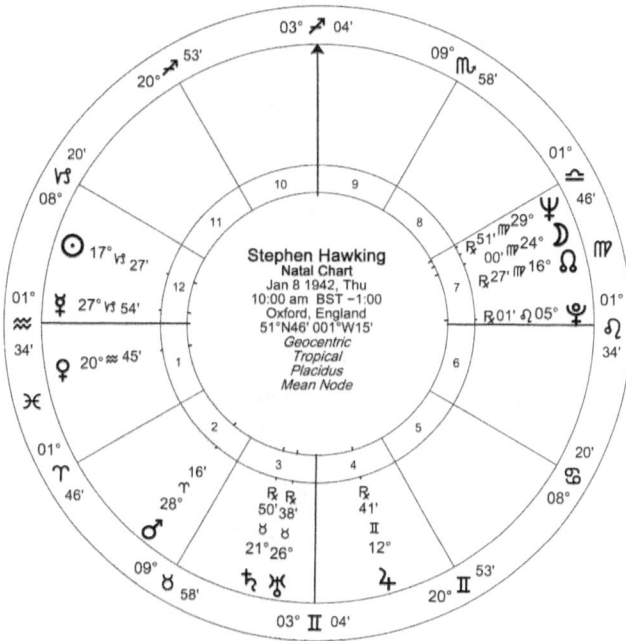

with scientific intuition. Einstein had Neptune in an earth sign trine Uranus in his chart, with Neptune ruling his Midheaven! Intuition can be a big part of scientific discoveries, which Hawking himself has talked about.

Stephen's Mercury is square Mars in his natal chart. The lure of the grand trine might be suspected of having the power to keep him from taking risks, from fulfilling his Mars in Aries need to make things happen. The trine could have the tendency, if he lets it, to lull his Mercury to sleep, and keep it within the bounds of the approved Capricorn suppositions. Mercury is square Mars for a reason, and the feeling in his youth (of that square) would have been anxiety about stepping outside the box of the mental constructs. His very intellectual father, according to Stephen, insisted on staying within proven boundaries; this was because his father had much experience with the non-risk-taking medical field. You don't take risks with people.

Emotional Dimensions of Astrology

But something happened to force Stephen out of dependence on the seductive grand trine. He lost normal self-sufficiency. At age twenty-one, in 1963, solar arc Mercury arrived to conjunct Steven's natal Venus, which was in a square with Saturn. This was in essence two feeling realms coming together for the first time in his life. It packed a punch. He was diagnosed with a neuron disease just months before he was to marry his first wife.

Venus square Saturn is one of the most significant feeling realms that we can experience in life (along with the conjunction and opposition of those two). Anyone who has it knows the depth to which we must go in order to be in true union with another person. The feelings that come to our attention with this configuration expand the length and breadth of all possibilities in a relationship with someone. It would be a mistake to think that Saturn trine Venus is for those who have mastered love by previously living a successful version of the square between Saturn and Venus. The trine is a glossy magazine cover compared with the hard aspect.

At age twenty-one Stephen was in love, like so many other males. The shock of hearing his diagnosis was a rude awakening. It wasn't just that he now faced disability. It was the sudden awareness of his original feelings about lovability and his doubt that he was in any way able to respond to love. It was also about his feelings of being inadequate in the scientific community, of being unsure of his ideas, unable to implement them with bravery (Mercury square Mars). It was forcing him to look at his life with no illusions.

He tried to push his girlfriend away but she was having none of it, and they married. A Saturn-Venus hard aspect always expects to earn love, and his girlfriend was offering him unconditional love, or so it must have seemed to him. Everything became a big question for him, and he needed to either give up or step up into a more mature version of his twenty-one-year-old self. So he stepped up.

I don't believe it was Stephen's grand trine that propelled him forward all these years in his life. It was the importance of love and the challenge of his physical limits, which had him questioning the limits of everything else (including God). That is what drove him forward in life. As Stephen himself said, "Before my condition was diagnosed, I was bored with life. There had not seemed to be anything worth doing."[15] It was only by living within his feeling realms and working on his important emotional structures that he was able to contribute what he has contributed to the world—the tireless presentation of research to others, and the example of fortitude in life.

As time went on, Hawking proved to be a man who did not insist on doing everything by himself, even in an intellectual way. He many times partnered with other scientists to work on ideas. He several times in his career came up with hypotheses that proved to be incorrect, and then later, not only recanted his statements but worked to see why they were not correct. This demonstrates his choice to bypass the defense mechanism formed by the grand trine, and move into the tension of Mercury square Mars. He was taking risks.

In 1974, when solar arc Sun was conjunct his natal Venus, highlighting his sense of wanting compliance with others, Stephen produced a paper on the disintegration of black holes, though he had previously stated that black holes could never get any smaller. Now he was saying otherwise. This was a beautiful bit of emotional integration for himself, in ways he may not have been fully aware of, allowing himself to be responsible for his mistakes, even while asking for the help of others.

In 1987, with solar arc Pluto opposing his Venus, Hawking got help so that he could publish his book, *A Brief History of Time*. This was a difficult time for him, pushing himself to the limit to prove his worth, and already knowing for years that his

---

[15]From "Overcoming Obstacles: Stephen Hawking," by Elizabeth Street on www.learningliftoff.com, January 8, 2015, retrieved April 2016.

wife Jane needed to have relief from the marriage. Although we don't know the half of what his life must have been like at the time, I cannot help but think that Hawking matured emotionally more than he is able to talk about.

Leo Buscaglia

Leo Buscaglia, a motivational speaker, teacher, and story teller, is a man who emotionally moved many people. He had a grand trine in fire between Mercury, Jupiter and Neptune. He could fire up a crowd with his inspiring stories, and then bring tears to their eyes. There was a second grand trine in his chart, in water—Moon, Saturn, Pluto, and South Node. Two grand trines! Thirty years ago, an astrologer would have said that Buscaglia was born with a silver tongue because of those two grand trines. However, there are many ways in which those grand trines could have been expressed, including the use of them for slick salesmanship. The content of his message was from decisions he made during his life, and from work within his feeling realms.

The first feeling realm in Leo's chart is the foundation of trust, the lunar nodes, which are in the third and ninth houses and with the Moon in Pisces. The suggestion is that Leo could trust in life as long as he could communicate to the public (Moon) his ideas and beliefs, especially that which brings unity or compassion. That could be anything. The real tension in his life is the hard aspects between his Sun, Pluto, and Mars. This is a very strong feeling realm.

We could say that Leo's feelings about standing up for himself in life were challenged by his feelings of taking action against powerful and hidden forces. Anybody with Mars in fourth harmonic aspect to Pluto has the feeling that they may not be able to take control of situations and they often end up feeling that their actions will be ineffective. However, there is great pressure to take action. When it involves the Sun, pride also comes under attack. This configuration suggests forces in the early home that

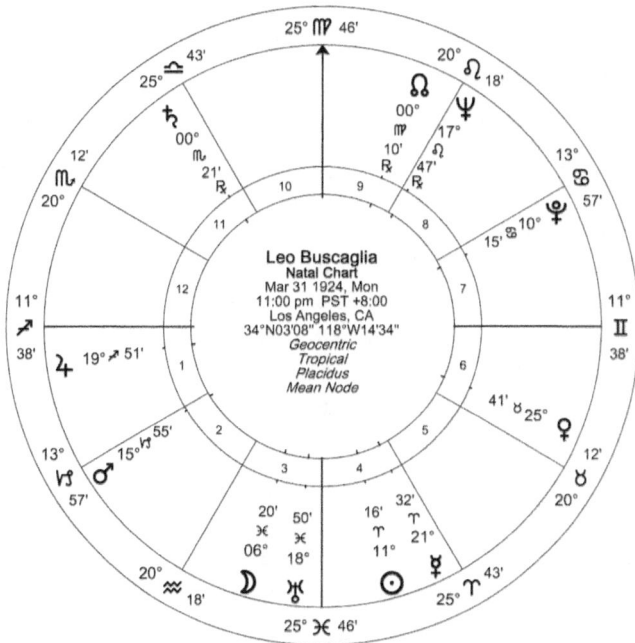

did not allow for autonomy. Someone in the home was a despot, probably the father.

Buscaglia rarely mentioned his father in the family stories he told. When he did, it was always with respect for one of his attributes. However, Leo related stories of his mamma many times, to share how she was passionate, compassionate, inspiring, and wise. If an astrologer were in consultation with Buscaglia, we would need to ask him about his father, and the feeling of being overwhelmed with the need to take action and effect change. We would ask how this was the key to acquiring his self-dignity.

We can see so well in the chart Leo's perception of his mother taking on the role of the father (Moon trine Saturn), and for accepting responsibility for what the father could have been, or wanted to be, within the family. The Moon aspect is an attempt to smooth over the Pluto-Sun square. The mother was working to show Leo that it was best to have compassion for the overbearing father who in fact was doing the best he could, even if he was making life difficult for everyone else.

Mars in Buscaglia's chart ruled the fifth house, which adds to the outgoing nature of Mars, and as a young boy the tension would naturally be released through sports and play; but Pluto ruled the twelfth house of things that are locked away and removed from everyday life. As Leo grew older he understood his need to dramatize and create ideas through story sharing, and he discovered his need to include the twelfth house dynamic in his life, which in this case is the forgotten people. He became a professor of special education, focusing on people who have fallen through the cracks of society.

The story of Buscaglia as Dr. Love is that in the late 1960s a student in one of his university classes committed suicide. This affected him deeply because he felt that he had missed an opportunity to help someone who was right in front of him.

I calculated the solar arcs that occurred in Leo's chart in the fall of 1969. (I don't have the exact date of the student's suicide.) On October 1 that year, the solar arc lunar nodes were at 16 Aries-Libra 03, just six weeks after they had formed a square with natal Mars at 15 Capricorn 55. Remember that an event can be expected three months prior to three months after the exact contact made by solar arcs, and sometimes it is a wider gap than that.

This suggests that there was a dynamic need for connection with his students that year through action taken. Also, fewer than three months from October 1, solar arc Venus would conjunct natal Pluto. In tandem with that, solar arc Sun would conjunct natal Venus—exactly in October of that year, so, yes, the Sun and Pluto were equidistant from Venus, and Venus is the midpoint between the two. This was something very powerful, so powerful, that we don't even need to look at transits for meaning.

However, I will look at transits, because it will confirm the solar arcs. Transiting Pluto was conjunct his Midheaven at 25 Virgo during October 1969, and his reputation, his career, was transformed into something more than a college professor. After the suicide incident, Buscaglia was seen around campus giving hugs, and he became known as Dr. Love.

Memories of the student suicide became part of Leo's emotional dimension in his Sun feeling realm. With the university's approval, he formed a new class, which did not give grades, and it was called "Love 1A". He lectured more and more for those who wanted to hear him speak. As time went on, his popularity grew, and his talks were seen all the time on public television. He wrote books. He didn't do it overnight, but he used the painful event in the fall of 1969 as an opportunity do his own emotional work. (Chart Data, A Rating)

Bobby Fischer

There is no one magic formula or perfect horoscope; we all have the perfect horoscope for ourselves. We each work with what we need, although some of us don't seem to gain a foothold in our own lives, even when we see an astrologer. If a grand trine is a blessing, there are many who are not aided by its good fortune. Bobby Fischer, often considered the greatest chess player of all time, was born with a grand trine in air signs. He certainly had a fine mind, but in the end it turned against him and he became delusional and paranoid.

In Fischer's horoscope we see Mars, Uranus, and Neptune in a close grand trine relationship. Mars rules Fischer's Midheaven so we see that the grand trine has everything to do with his career. Mars is on his Descendant, and any planet on an angle deserves special attention. The Descendant represents our "open enemies"; that is, our obvious opponents. Pluto sits near Bobby's Ascendant, defending it. It all looks like great strategy for a chess player.

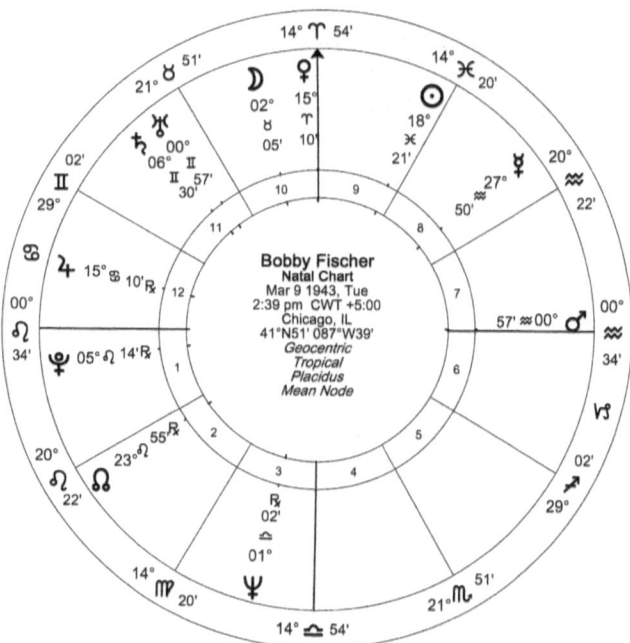

Even though Mars is in a grand trine, it is also in a fourth harmonic aspect with Pluto and the Moon, and that was a strong feeling realm for Bobby growing up. As a game, Mars in Aquarius on the Descendant might keep its head, stay cool, and use the support it gets from Neptune and Uranus. Uranus can help with surprise attacks, and Neptune can help with sneak attacks. It is strategic. But Mars within the feeling realm with the Moon is not going to be the cool responder, not even in Aquarius.

Fischer had neither a father who was willing to publicly claim him as son, nor a mother who was warm and nurturing. His mother was a brilliant woman who, because of social circumstances during WWII, was required to make her own way as a single mom with two children. She was independent, political, and professionally ambitious. By the time Bobby was age sixteen and completely obsessed with playing chess, his mother had moved out of their apartment to attend medical school, leaving him to fend for himself. Bobby was already an emotionally deprived child, and at age sixteen, practically an orphan.

Regina, his mother, who like Bobby had Mercury conjunction the South Node (born March 31, 1913), passed on to him the need to use his mental faculties in order to trust in life and get along with others. Nothing fit Fischer better than having a partner or opponent who could challenge his thinking skills. However, his Mercury and the lunar nodes are complicated by their square to Uranus. We could say that Bobby's mother gave him an extraordinary challenge to be mentally unique in the world.

The Moon in hard aspect to Mars and Pluto is, however, the most challenging feeling realm in Bobby's chart, and therefore would be the most important source for understanding himself. I don't believe that he ever understood himself or directly worked with his own emotions. He spent his whole life immersing himself in his grand trine aspect as an escape from the pain of his feeling realms. There was no one in his life to help him understand. He had an extraordinary need to be nurtured, but there were things being hidden from him, and his identity was in question.

Bobby's Sun was not in any fourth harmonic aspects, so we can assume that he was told things about his father that satisfied his ego or otherwise made him feel special. The Sun trine retrograde Jupiter in the twelfth house suggests pride in a father who was prominent but hidden, almost non-existent. Paul Nemenyi (born, June 5, 1895), the physicist who likely was Bobby's father, has natal Jupiter just five degrees from Jupiter in Bobby's chart. Nemenyi also has a lunar node conjunction Bobby's Sun. It would have made so much sense if he had acknowledged Bobby as his son and took credit and responsibility for his young life.

There is plenty of evidence that Bobby knew Paul was his father[16], but he was not allowed to declare it. He was required

---

[16]From "Life is not a board game" by Peter Nicholas, *Philadelphia Inquirer*, February 9, 2001.

Emotional Dimensions of Astrology

to protect his mother and himself from gossip and scandal. So, while on the one hand, Bobby could feel good about having a prominent scientist for a father, he was disallowed from extending that fact into social recognition. It must have been very frustrating for him.

Jupiter in Fischer's horoscope is square Venus at the Midheaven. While the square of Jupiter to Venus can express itself as social overconfidence, the feeling of it as a child is much more complex. For Bobby as a young person, he could have felt that being compliant was a pretense, a show, a coverup, for the missing father in the home (Venus rules the fourth house). Perhaps Bobby felt he was merely his father's "charity" case since he hardly ever saw him and his mother received money for his care.

The T-square between Moon, Pluto, and Mars is where all of Bobby's feelings landed. Like Buscaglia, Fischer experienced deep frustrations about effecting action against forces that were hidden and powerful, but in Bobby's case it had much to do with being nurtured since it concerned his Moon function. Bobby could perhaps manage to excuse his father for not taking full responsibility of him, but he could not forgive his mother for not giving him the sort of nurturing a young child needs. In fact, he probably never even sorted it out in his mind.

Except when Fischer was very young, age two to three, he did not experience any hard solar arc aspects to his Moon feeling realm until age seventeen in 1960. There were plenty of transits and plenty of experiences before then that fleshed out the Moon feeling realm, but no large events that created the memories needed to develop the emotional dimensions there. In March 1960, solar arc Venus and solar arc Jupiter made exact fourth harmonic contact with the natal Moon, one conjunction and one square to it. Already recognized worldwide for his gaming genius, Bobby experienced his first and only big failure at chess at a tournament in Buenos Aires that began March 29, 1960. It was said that he lost his concentration and lost his virginity, distracted by a star-struck young lady[17] who captured his attention at the tournament. He would never again let someone distract him like that.

Since he was seventeen and unsupervised, this was to be expected; but it was more than just a tabloid event for him. Venus awakened the emotions within the Moon realm. It was a matter of one feeling realm encountering another one, and was not just a blow to his career. It was a cruel reminder to him that Venus was indeed the great pretender, overblown and dangerous. It is significant to see that at the beginning of March that year, transiting Saturn reached 15 Capricorn and was square the Venus feeling realm. It seems that he never felt less loved than during that time in Argentina.

It was not until 1974, when Fischer was thirty-one, that there was another solar arc to his Moon feeling realm. Again, there were plenty of other measurements before that, plenty of opportunities for emotional growth, but solar arcs are the best markers for activation. In early July 1974, Neptune arrived by solar arc to an opposition with the Moon, and this, in fact, turned out to be the beginning of the end for Bobby's ability to react in less than logical ways, without adding in some sort of paranoid suspicion to it.

Bobby had for years made personal demands at tournaments. He won the title of World Champion in 1972 in Iceland against the Soviet chess master Spassky while being given special treatment and accommodated with a private room for one of the matches.

At the end of June 1974, Bobby was told that if he wanted to defend his title the following year, he had to sign an agreement. He made a list of demands, and the chess congress voted against accommodating him. In addition to the solar arc of Neptune to the Moon, transiting Jupiter was conjunct Bobby's Sun, reflecting the extra ego-mania. The solar arc of doubt was remedied

---

[17]From *The King*; see bibliography.

by false pride! Fischer chose to withdraw from the competition.

After that he became increasingly odd, withdrawn, and disagreeable, and began to think that he was being watched. Even though he had Jewish origins, he began to hate all Jews and announced that they were dangerous. He didn't feel safe.

The bigger truth in all this is that Fischer had never felt safe. Pluto on the Ascendant is in a defensive position for good reason, counteracting Mars on the Descendant feeling that he was always under attack. As long as he was engaging in a chess game, he could win on some level and feel empowered. But it did not engage his emotional realm enough. It was only life in an intellectual grand trine, in the world of a game. Life was pretend, just like love.

It could have been all so different. In 1960, when Bobby was seventeen, when he was distracted by his sexual interlude, he had no one to talk with about it. It took on mammoth proportions because it was stored as an emotional dimension full of hurt and confusion, and categorized as a detriment. What should have been something meaningful to him, even as a lesson, became a threat to his defense system.

That is the danger of a grand trine. When a person feels that the grand trine is a savior, the truth is just the opposite: it is a trap. Grand trines do not save, and they can take us away from our true selves. There are lots of ways we could imagine Bobby Fischer working through his emotional dimensions to bring maturity and growth, but it didn't happen. After 1974, Bobby made a couple of comebacks to the chess scene, but mostly he lived in self-exile around the world, and there were many reports of his erratic and paranoid behavior. He was not a fully functioning human being, only one who was broken and afraid. (Data Rating: B; rectified by the author)

Chapter 10

Matching Feeling Realms

"Marriage, like a submarine, is only safe if you get all the way inside."—Frank Pittman

A very pronounced premise within astrology is that compatibility between two people is best when there are flowing aspects between them, such as trines and sextiles, and sometimes conjunctions, depending upon which planets. Particularly in amorous relationships, one person's Mars conjunction the other person's Venus does seem to work for attraction and sexual similitude. If Mercury signs are in compatible elements, communication will have less friction, but not always. Supposedly, with two incompatible elements, communication can get spoiled before the understanding is obtained. However, that can occur anyway, and it all comes down to whether the two people have a good amount of maturity.

People always need to work on their emotional dimensions in life if they expect to engage in a relationship. Having a feeling realm that touches another person's feeling realm does not usually result in friendship or romance, but it happens. It is not accidental; nor are the two people purposefully punishing themselves. They have found someone who understands them. This can be good or bad. Sharing memories (through transits) can also be extremely helpful to these individuals to act as a couple.

Unfortunately there can be a negative use for this, such as people who seem to give support to each other where there should be no support, such as in a co-dependent relationship. Political couples and criminals might find it helpful. Bill Clinton, for instance, has a Sun- Moon square where Hillary has a Mercury-Saturn square, and it also includes her lunar nodes. Where he has a need to work on his self-nurturing versus his self-dignity, she has a need to work on her communication boundaries. This could be a good thing. But according to some popular opinion, it appears that the two of them tend to cover up each other's weaknesses.

My husband and I don't have any matching feeling realms in our charts. We have trines and sextiles to each other's horoscopes, and we have one exact conjunction between his Jupiter and my Mars. So when transits come around to that point, things happen (of course things happen), but those times are not part of our emotional dimensions.

It is very brave for people to try to work together on their most difficult areas in life. Below are presented stories of couples who had shared feeling realm points. Sometimes when significant transits arrived at those points, they were amazingly also accompanied by solar arcs in each individual chart, but that is an extra "coincidence." You obviously cannot count on them. In any case, it might be helpful to use these examples to see how some people have managed to connect with another person in a soul-building capacity, using their deepest feelings; or at least, the opportunity to do that.

Simone de Beauvoir and Jean Paul Sarte

Jean Paul Sartre (previously discussed in chapter 2) was a philosopher and writer obsessed with the concept of personal intellectual freedom (Gemini Sun quendecile the Ascendant). He had a conjunction in his horoscope between Sun, Mercury, and Pluto in Gemini. With the conjunction we feel the pressure of the need for control over our mental processing, especially since it is in Gemini. The sign Gemini encourages experimentation and variety, while the function of Pluto is to seek a place to anchor and to concentrate energy into a deep place.

Jean Paul's need to converse about life and to consider the very processes of thinking was in essence his need to work on his feelings about relationships (Mercury-ruled Descendant), and his feelings about sex (Sun-ruled eighth house), and his feelings about immersion in the depths of society (Pluto-ruled eleventh and twelfth houses). It is no wonder he chose not to marry, choosing freedom over commitment. It was apparently a very painful and personal task for him to have a relationship with a person.

Simone de Beauvoir, the woman who was Jean Paul's constant companion for many years, had Pluto two degrees from Jean Paul's Pluto. She had a square from Pluto to a stellium of Saturn, Mars, and Moon in Pisces at the Nadir. Before we talk about what this intersection might bring them as a couple, we'll look at what it brought Simone as an individual.

De Beauvoir is most known for her views on women and gender equality, and is the author of *The Second Sex* (1949). In her own words, she quoted her father saying one time, "Simone thinks like a man!"[18], and she declared that she admired her father for his individualism, as opposed to her mother's conventional Catholicism. If she resented her mother's conservatism, she nevertheless was quite influenced by her as well, since we see the Moon Nodes in her horoscope in a large stellium with the Sun, Mercury, Neptune, and Uranus. We can say that Simone could trust in life as long as she could shine in her intuitive and unique thinking capacity about deep matters of self-worth.

It seems that Simone acquired her faith in her unique and clear thinking, her trust in life, from her mother, and not as much from her father. Perhaps the mother pushed too hard, and

---
[18]"Introduction," *The Second Sex*, Judith Thurman, 2010.

challenged her too much with all the religious dogma, because it backfired. It took root well enough at first. Simone wanted to be a nun until she was fourteen, at which time she said she suddenly became an atheist.

The feeling realm of Saturn-Mars-Moon square Pluto involves a sexual overtone, if not actual sexual trauma for Simone. Mars rules the fifth house and the Moon rules the eighth house, and they are close to each other in degree. The feelings of self-worth are involved because Saturn rules the second house. Simone's need to nurture herself with assertion was extraordinary in nature and was in tension with the feeling of wanting to gain control over herself and over others (remember the adrenalin Moon of Mars square Moon?). All of it was in direct contact with Jean Paul's feeling realm about his own relationships and sexual intimacy.

At age seven Simone received her first trigger to that feeling realm with a solar arc of Saturn to the Moon (conjunction) in early June 1915. Also, a solar arc of Pluto had arrived at the Aries Point the year earlier. Anytime a planet makes a solar arc to an Aries Point, some manifestation of that planet occurs out of its original position. In Simone's case, the Pluto in Gemini in the seventh house was ready to deliver an important message. In addition to the solar arcs mentioned, there was a transiting Uranus-Venus conjunction, also exact in early June 1915.

Only Simone could tell us exactly what happened that year. The need to be individually valued (Saturn ruling the second house) interfered with her need to be valuable with others (Moon ruling the eighth house). For a seven-year-old, this is the feeling of possibly being "used." It may not have been in a sexual way, but it was at least in a way that seemed derogatory to a little girl. She no doubt, considering who she was, already noticed that boys were not used in the same way as girls, and certainly not for just being cute.

Later, at age fourteen, Simone had a second hit to her feeling realms, a solar arc of the Moon to 14 Aries, square her lunar nodal axis at 14 Capricorn-Cancer. This was the age at which she said she suddenly became an atheist because of something that happened, and it would have been a particular offense against the mother. Over the course of that year we see the normal Saturn opposition to Saturn, which is the usual adolescent rebellion, and then Saturn transiting opposition her Moon in the summer. The implications can go into the sexual area once again, simply because the Moon rules the eighth house, and we can infer that there was rebellion against the mother because of it.

It is safe to say that Simone could have had a sexual encounter with another female at that age, and been caught, although she might have put it in her memoirs if that were true. If something like that happened, or indeed with a boy, maybe the father defended her against the mother, suggesting that it was all quite normal curiosity. Later in life Simone was promiscuously bi-sexual. In fact, Simone was accused of seducing many underage female students when she taught at university, and then of sharing her romantic discards with Jean Paul. She was introducing them, and selecting women for seduction by Jean Paul.[19] He was also doing very well on his own finding romantic partners.

For obvious reasons, Sartre was very involved in Simone's private emotional work about her sexuality, as she was involved with his. His Pluto-Mercury was busy psychoanalyzing every relationship with Simone. He witnessed it through her, and then tried it on for size for himself. Since the legal age of sexual consent in Paris was older than some of the girls that Simone chose to seduce, we can wonder about the morality of these two people. From their point of view they were just practicing their newly found existential beliefs. They believed that they hadn't really hurt anyone because the young women were free to decide for themselves. Dealing with the consequences of all of that was confrontation, and they eventually publicly contested the law and rallied for reform.

---
[19] *Tete-a-tete: Simone de Beauvoir and Jean Paul Sartre*; see bibliography.

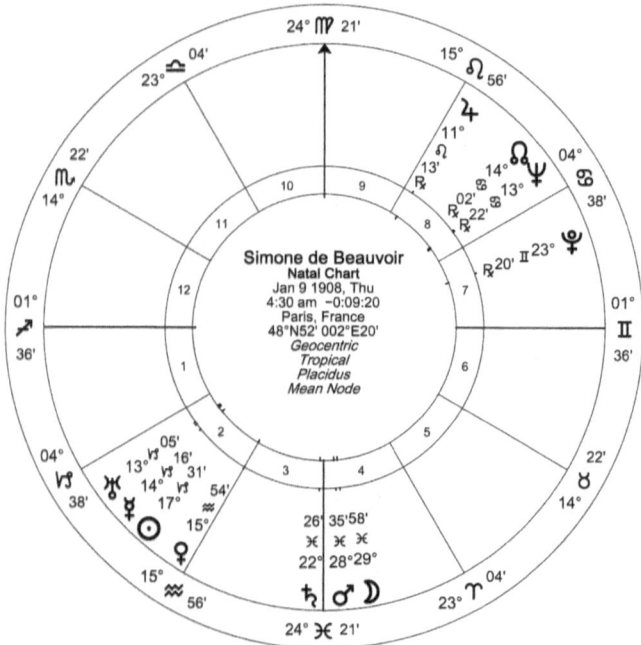

Sartre's Sun in his feeling realm was exactly square Simone's Moon, ruler of her eighth house (feelings about blending her worth with that of others). His Sun ruled his eighth house (as an intercepted sign). Sartre's Pluto, and also Simone's Pluto, ruled both of their twelfth houses—the feeling of taking care of humanity at large, or blending with others behind the scenes. For them, the things they felt were so much about freedom of expression, particularly in relationships, and about things they thought were innately applicable to everyone, and to everyone's health and well-being. Perhaps it was a fault of having their particular feeling realms so complicit that they validated each other's dilemmas. In spite of these feeling realms being very personal to them, they acted as if it were everyone's dilemma.

In 1943, Simone wrote and published a novel about a romantic relationship between three people, *She Came to Stay*. It was based on two sisters that Simone and Jean Paul had become in-

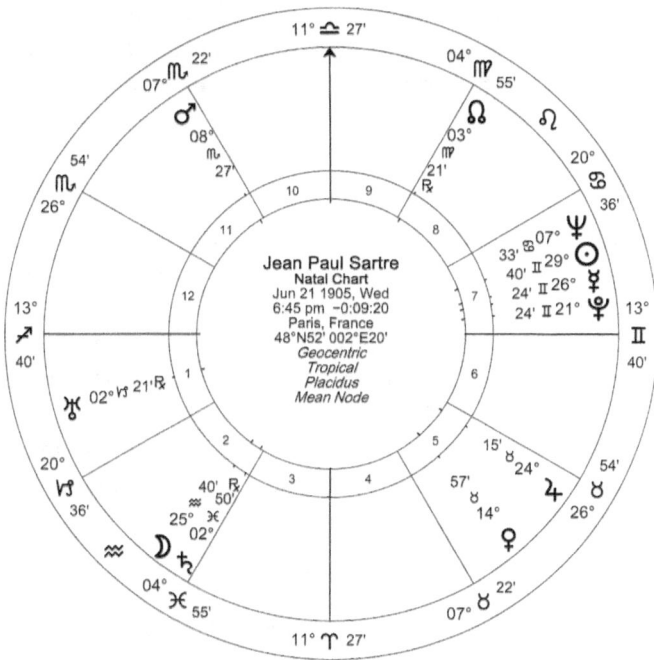

volved with, so in reality there were four people rather than the three in the book. The book was not well liked, but it is a study of Jean Paul and Simone's relationship. At the time Simone wrote it, there were solar arcs in both Simone and Jean Paul's charts. A solar arc of Venus made a conjunction to Simone's Saturn at 22 Pisces; and in Jean Paul's chart, a solar arc of Venus made a conjunction to Pluto at 21 Gemini. This was extraordinary! At the same time, in the summer of 1943, transiting Neptune arrived at 29 Virgo, so it was opposition Simone's Moon, and square Jean Paul's Sun.

If ever there was a time when two people could work on their feeling realms together, this was it, which of course goes to say that both Simone and Jean Paul were deeply affected by the affair with these two women. One of the sisters in this complex relationship has a published birth date (November 6, 1915) and we can see that her Mars and lunar nodes are aligned with Sim-

Emotional Dimensions of Astrology

one's natal Venus, her Mars exactly opposition Simone's Venus. I rather believe that it was Jean Paul who was inordinately jealous of the relationship between Simone and this woman. He tried to have an affair with her, but she rejected him, and so instead he had an affair with her younger sister. Later he financially supported both of them for years.

What he and Simone learned is hard to say, and whether they experienced soul growth is anybody's guess, although I haven't read all the correspondences that Simone later published. Jean Paul would have said that it didn't matter, that there was no purpose or continuance of his life, only what was authentic at the time. Simone was much the same, of course, and if they found a path into themselves through their time together, I'm unaware of it. However, it seems that they tried. (Data Rating, de Beauvoir, AA; Data Rating, Sarte, AA)

Humphrey Bogart and Lauren Bacall

Almost everyone knows their names. They made four movies together, and had two children. They each had four planets in their mutable and mutual feeling realms, and Bogart's included his lunar nodal axis. Bacall's Jupiter was conjunction Humphrey's Mercury (one degree), and the rest of her planets were in square aspect to Bogart's planets, some closer in orb than others, but certainly a significant set of squares. Like Sartre and de Beauvoir, the mutable feeling realms in their charts were about communication. Both Bacall and Bogart were famous for the delivery of their lines. Bacall even deliberately altered the tone of her voice for maximum effect. Unlike Sartre and de Beauvoir, it was the male of the couple who had the most complex and difficult feeling realm.

Both of the horoscopes have been rectified to the times given here through my study of events in their lives. I won't go through the process, though I can tell you it was not a guess. However, regardless of correct times of birth, the discussion here will

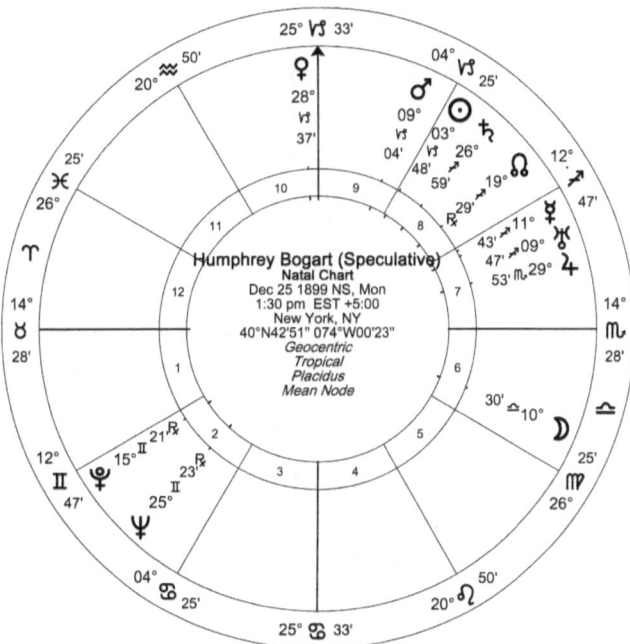

emphasize the function of the planets involved, rather than the houses they rule, along with information we know about these two people.

Lauren was twenty-five years younger than Humphrey Bogart. When they married, she was twenty and he was forty-five. It didn't seem to matter in Hollywood. Bogart had a passion for assertive women, and Lauren fit the bill. With her Aries Moon, she was not going to take orders, and although Bogart liked giving orders, he thought it was all part of the fun to argue. Having verbal arguments about things was natural for them, and their Mercury placements were square, hers in Virgo and his in Sagittarius. Where his thoughts came to judge swiftly with Sagittarius, her thoughts matched his in speed (the accompanying Uranus) but with greater practical application since it was in an earth sign.

The arguing worked perfectly well in the movies, given their sarcastic and biting lines, but you have to wonder how it sorted itself out in real life. Actors Katherine Hepburn and Spencer Tracy had similar mutable and mutual feeling realms, but they never married to each other. They only argued in the movies.

To understand what these feeling realms are about, we need to look back at their beginnings. Bogart's parents were successful at what they did for a living. His father was an accomplished doctor, and his mother was an illustrator who made more money than his father did. Bogart's lunar nodal axis had Pluto on one side of it, and Neptune opposed by Saturn on the other. This describes Bogart's trust in life—his hard work to create his art and his powerful communication. His mother showed him how.

Bogart shared with the public that his mother was not affectionate, not even a little bit.[20] For him, verbal communication was everything, and he did not like being touched in ordinary affectionate ways. He wasn't accustomed to it. With so much pressure on communication, he felt he must get it right. Mercury was the only personal planet in his feeling realm set. Mercury was with Uranus, Pluto, Neptune, the Nodes, and Saturn. This was an extraordinary amount of need to communicate dynamically.

When Bogart and Bacall married on May 21, 1945, transiting Uranus was at 12 Gemini, an approximate half cycle for Bogie (the mid-life crisis), and a little less than a quarter cycle for Bacall. Uranus was opposition her Jupiter and square her Mercury. In addition, transiting Jupiter was at 17 Virgo. Six months prior there was a solar arc at the time of her lunar node square Jupiter from 12 Pisces 26, and this brought her mother into her daughter's wedding plans, as well as the public at large. Later that year, Bogart had his own solar arc Venus square his Pluto.

These two actors stayed together for the rest of Bogart's life, which ended in 1957 with esophageal cancer. It is not a surprise

---

[20]*A Life in Hollywood*; see bibliography

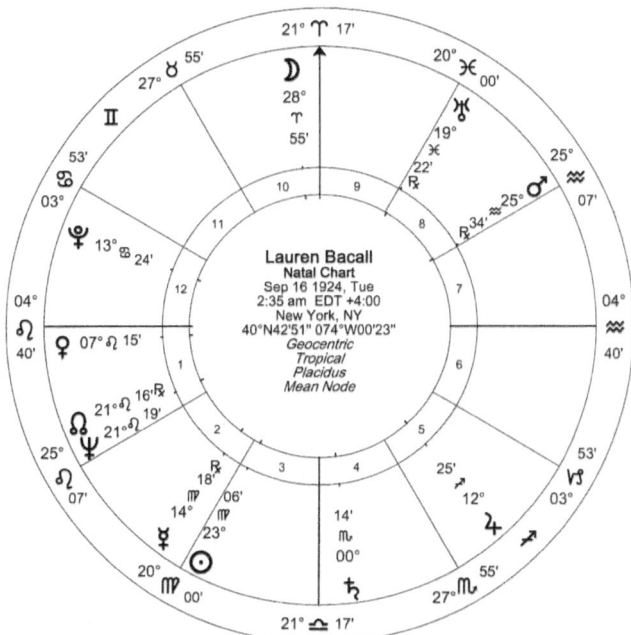

that it was his throat that failed. It was attributed to his smoking habit, but in another realm of thinking, smoke is a way of coating or camouflaging the throat for not saying everything that needs to be said in just the right way.

Lauren had aspects in her chart that suggested she also felt unloved early in life. Her Venus square Saturn required emotional work. Her parents were divorced when she was very young, and she did not stay in contact with her father. Her mother took on the father's role, and we see Saturn opposition Moon, so we can suppose that the mother managed and Lauren respected her for it. This alone would compel a woman to be forthcoming with her words, to not hold back with her opinions.

The T-square of Mercury opposition Uranus square Jupiter in Sagittarius represented an extraordinary need in Bacall's life to voice her opinions. Unlike Bogart, Lauren had encouragement and support from her mother. I can't help but think that Lau-

Emotional Dimensions of Astrology   157

ren's emotional growth flourished during her marriage to Bogie, and that Bogart's task was harder work for him than it was for her. He found the perfect person to help him, and perhaps his children know how much he matured during his life together with Bacall. (Chart Data: Bacall, B; Bogart, speculative)

Marie and Pierre Curie

This is another pair of people whose names are internationally known. Marie was the first woman to receive a Nobel Prize. She received it with her husband and one other male scientist. It was Marie, however, who had persisted with the specific research that led to their prize. This persistence was in keeping with the feeling realms that matched between she and Pierre—in fixed signs, the signs that are most insistent on strength of presence in life. The motto of the fixed mode should be "I am." If it takes work to get there, so be it, but the mode is the one that establishes dominance and power through the effort of *being*.

Pierre's feeling realm that matches Marie's is a simple trust situation. He has the lunar nodes at 25 Aquarius-Leo, and the Sun at 23 Taurus 41. His need (an extraordinary one) is to shine for his scientific discoveries at his workplace for the benefit of everyone in the world. His Sun ruled the sixth house of giving service, and the lunar nodes were located in the sixth and twelfth houses. This is his primary feeling realm, and he must accommodate it somehow. Perhaps he chose Marie because he felt her own extraordinary needs in life would not interfere with his needs, and would even enhance them.

We could say that Marie was more driven than Pierre, and she engaged him through his zodiac degrees, which he understood completely. Marie's Venus-Saturn conjunction was a close one, Saturn at 25 Scorpio 16, and Venus at 25 Scorpio 26, and they were in a square with Pierre's lunar nodal axis at 25 Aquarius-Leo, and so also opposition his Sun. Her Mars was at 29 Scorpio 37, and Jupiter at 28 Aquarius 00, so we see the abundance of determination resonating with Pierre's simpler needs in that area.

Aside from these squares we see in late fixed signs between the two, we also see that Marie had a middle Scorpio Sun opposed by a middle Taurus Pluto, and Pierre had an early Scorpio Moon opposed by an early Taurus Pluto, and square Saturn in Leo. Where Marie's feeling realm concerns her dignity and pride, Pierre had a feeling realm that concerned his ability to nurture himself and others.

Growing up in the Curie household, Pierre and his brother were educated by their father, a medical doctor. Both boys had an aptitude for science and mathematics. Nevertheless, their horoscopes suggest it was the mother in their life who provided them with the incentive to move forward and excel in life. Both brothers had strong lunar nodal axes. Jacques, also a scientist (born October 29, 1856), had the lunar nodes conjunction-opposition Mercury and square retrograde Saturn.

The function of thinking must have been extremely important to the mother, and she was the person in charge of the rules in the household (Saturn with Moon in one child's chart, and with the lunar nodes in the other child's chart). Pierre's most fundamental feeling realm was to be noticed as a shining intellectual who helps others. His strong secondary feeling realm (Moon opposition Pluto, which his brother also had) was much more challenging to accommodate. In fact, it was too handy for him to just let Marie own that energy, to represent it for him.

When Pierre and Marie were married in July 1895, transiting Mars was at 28 Leo, opposition Marie's Jupiter. They both had marriage-related solar arcs, but those were not part of the feeling realms mentioned here. However, transiting Mars was stimulating their feeling realms, and when they took their wedding vows they also were swearing to be partners in research. Marie helped Pierre make a name for himself, and she helped him fulfill his lunar nurturing need by being his companion in the lab, and of course by bearing his children.

Emotional Dimensions of Astrology

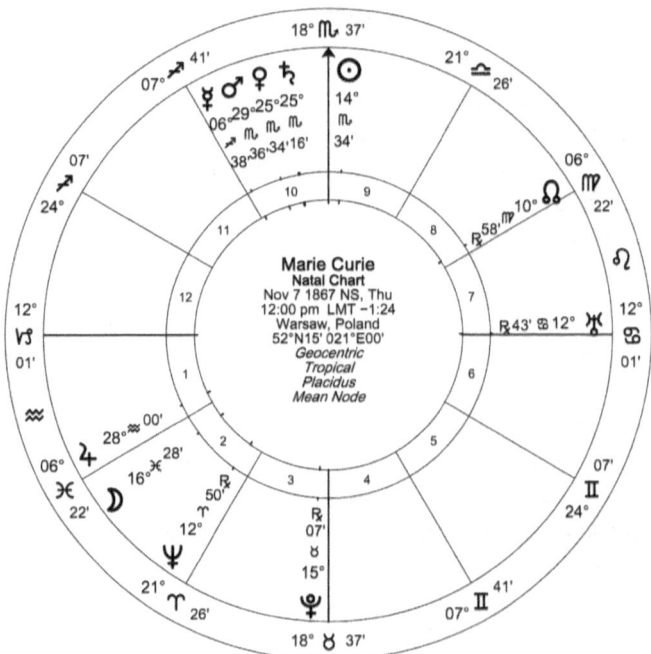

Of the two, I think Marie had the more challenging circumstances in her life, beginning with her early home. Her father and mother, who had both been respected teachers in Poland (in a Russian enclave of Warsaw), had fallen from status and financial security after a political coup of sorts, and they suffered greatly because of it. When Marie was only ten years old, her mother, who had keenly felt this fall from grace, died of tuberculosis in November 1877. At the time in Marie's chart, there was a solar arc of Pluto opposition Saturn at 25 Scorpio. This was two feeling realms coming together, as we saw occurring with the examples of Bobby Fischer, Stephen Hawking, and others.

In Marie's horoscope, Pluto ruled the Midheaven, which often represents a parent, especially in youth, and Saturn ruled the Ascendant. This was all about identity requiring transformation through the ultimate effect of death. Remember that solar arc Pluto was also square Jupiter, co-ruler of the first house, transit-

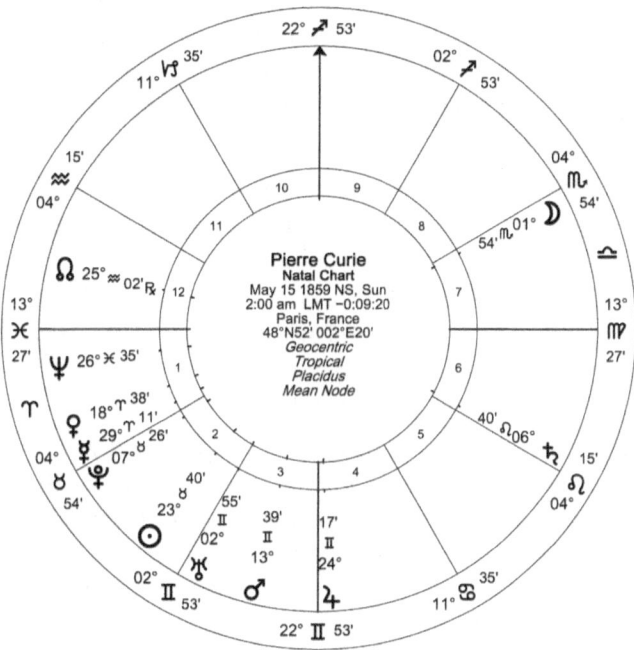

ing Pluto was opposition Venus, which ruled the fourth house of home, and transiting Uranus arrived at 25 Leo. After that, the solar arc of the Sun would do the same thing. This was overwhelming for a young girl. It was not just losing a mother, but being handed the giant task of redeeming the status and dignity of the family's legacy, probably something that seemed impossible.

These were horrific memories for Marie as an emotional dimension within her feeling realm of Venus-Saturn. Here was a strong woman with a fixed mode feeling realm, who took it upon herself to reacquire the status the family had lost and repair some of the damage that had been done to her family's efforts to build that reputation. It was an inherited circumstance that created the feeling that love and admiration must be earned.

As she and Pierre worked within their emotional dimensions to acquire the status they believed they needed, they were building their own emotional dimensions with shared memories. This must have helped Marie, and it must have been what they sometimes talked about—how it felt to them to be scientists who had acquired respect from their hard work and from their stunning contributions.

In late 1899, just before the turn of the century, transiting Jupiter crossed the degrees in Scorpio that triggered their feeling realm. At that time they published many scientific papers that led to their Nobel Prize in 1903, one of which was the fact that radiation reduced the size of tumor cells. This was scientific achievement, but it was also much more to them. They had fought for it with very emotional reasons.

Pierre and Marie understood one another, and not just because they both understood science. They worked for the same thing. They achieved the same thing, though it was only a last minute change of heart in the scientific community that honored the first woman with a Nobel Prize. She had earned it every step of the way, and Pierre knew it.

Marie ultimately died from her work, succumbing to radiation poisoning on July 4, 1934. Transiting Saturn at the time was just one degree from an exact conjunction to her natal Jupiter, and her solar arc Moon had arrived at her husband's natal Sun degree. He had perished in a road accident years prior. As with the example of Fred Rogers, Saturn marks a finishing point, a declaration of status achieved. It in some way shows that our time of death is meaningful, and that we have arrived at a natural ending point.(Chart Data: Pierre Curie, C, rectified; Marie Curie, AA)

Chapter 11

Emotional Places

"No matter where you go, there you are."—Yogi Berra

There are places in this world that hold emotional energy because of the things that occurred there, and because the emotion was strong enough to attach itself to the place, psychically and physically. Sure, every inch on this earth has seen tragedy and great joy, eons of times, but psychic afterglows thrive and eventually fade over time, and get replaced by something else that occurs or becomes the blend of emotions we feel every day. Often these places are where large numbers of people have been affected collectively. The places that hold historical significance are especially strong because they resonate with all of us, and obviously we go there to remember and give honor to those who were there, or to reflect on what occurred.

These places, like people, are defined emotionally by the hard aspects in the horoscope. The horoscope represents the event that makes the place what it still is today. Intuitive people will feel the impact of sorrow or fear or courage or love that lingers there. Others might feel it because the incident that marks it has a zodiacal degree that is an important one in their own chart, and so the resonance happens naturally without any contemplation. To come across a place that resonates with self is not incidental. It is a meaningful life event. If you live near such a place that holds collective emotion, you live there because you need to embrace more of that emotion to help you understand and grow. If you are on a trip or you go to a place with a friend, you can bet that it is the right time for you to be sharing in a particular kind of collective emotion.

Pearl Harbor

The chart of Pearl Harbor is a good example of a place that has been marked by unexpected loss of life. There are places that have suffered more, of course, such as in Germany and in Japan, such as Dresden and Hiroshima, not to mention the Jewish concentration camps. What was especially terrible about Pearl Harbor was that there was no threat or anticipation of attack. The sailors who worked on the carriers in the harbor were not prepared psychologically for an attack. Survivors reported that there was disbelief and shock when the attack came because it had never been imagined, nor was there any plan in place for the eventuality.

There are still 942 bodies interred in the sunken U.S.S. Arizona in the harbor. The memorial is a platform over the water that looks down on parts of the carrier that sunk to the bottom of the harbor. A short ferry ride takes visitors out to this platform, and people are asked to be respectful and quiet because it is a tomb. They needn't be reminded, for people are speechless, except for the occasional bewildered child who really just wants to go play in the water. People look down into the beautiful turquoise water and become reverent, thinking on their own good fortune, or the incongruity of the soft lapping of the water over the remnants of those who died screaming in anguish and shock.

The horoscope for the event reflects what happened that day. There is a grand fire trine, which surely must have been both the enemy attack and the sailors' quick responses. There were a lot of explosions and a lot of loss from fire. In spite of knowing that they would most likely die that day, the sailors took up arms

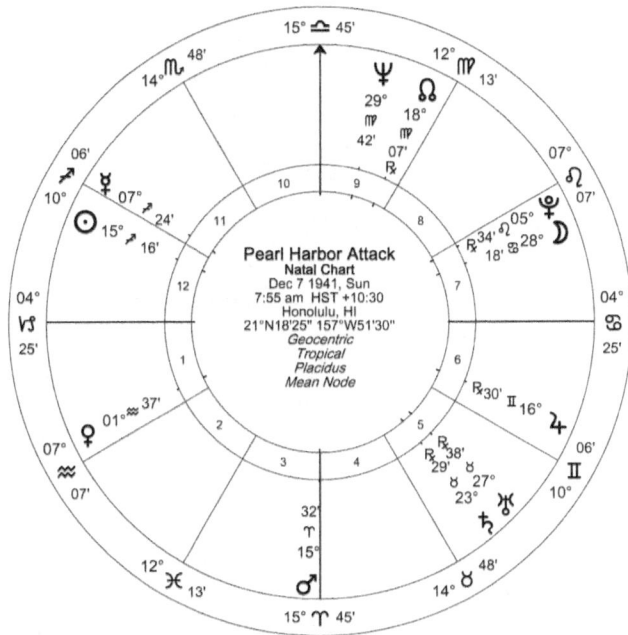

and did the best they could. So often a grand trine in fire allows a person to have free passage to inspiration and action, using whatever beliefs are available at the time to sustain it.

When the first assault came, Mars in Aries was on the fourth house cusp, the homeland. The carriers in the harbor were the homes of the sailors, at least for that while. The Sagittarius Sun was in the twelfth house, which is so often the house which holds a drowned person—someone who has disappeared. The eighth house, the house the Sun rules, the house of death, holds Chiron in Leo, the open wound of the hero that stays open forever because it has earned the honor. A grand trine is not considered a soul-building aspect, at least not by me, but it is beautiful energy for anyone who has made the decision to sacrifice his or her life for others or for an ideal.

The primary feeling realm in the horoscope is the lunar nodal axis, which is in a grand cross with a Sun-Jupiter opposition.

Emotional Dimensions of Astrology

That is the real feeling realm here. Notice that Jupiter rules the twelfth house, where we see the Sun already promised to the ocean. Jupiter is in the sixth house, the house of work and military service. There are many ways to look at this set, but we can say that there was trust at that time as long as they could fight together for what they believed in.

A second feeling realm was the Saturn-Uranus conjunction in Taurus in the fifth house. Saturn rules the Ascendant so it is the picture of the sailors under attack needing to improvise and come up with practical solutions. Proper equipment was not at the ready. Uranus ruled the second house of possessions. If a weapon didn't work, they had to find one that did. Many told afterwards that they shouted and worked together to do anything that would work. They fought with creativity and urgency.

The most painful emotional dimension in the chart is the Venus-Pluto opposition. With little time to think at all, it is amazing that someone would have time to think of a loved one, but they did. During trauma, during a time that leads to death, we go through remarkable things. We experience a mini-review of our life, of what has gone before . . . all in a flash! Time becomes a stretchy entity, and we recognize the importance of our emotions.

Venus, especially in Aquarius, is brotherly love. There was no particular hatred for the Japanese on any of those carriers prior to the event. The enemy was Japan, not the Japanese people who lived on the island. Afterwards, there was confinement of all Japanese males in the U.S, and eventually of whole Japanese families. Pluto energy can manifest negatively and be controlling. Pluto opposition Venus in the chart can also represent prophetically the nuclear event that would occur later, when the enemy would suffer horribly from a nuclear blast. The war inevitably unleashed the use of a weapon that changed the world forever.

It is only the harbor in Oahu that has been marked with this terrible incident. Honolulu is yet a place of joy, of play, and a regular mix of crime and chaos that all cities experience. If you go to Pearl Harbor, check your horoscope for resonance with the event chart. Say a prayer for those who died. A few of them might yet walk between worlds, on the decks or by the docks. They may not yet know what has happened to them. (Chart Data: AA Rating)

Woodstock

Shown here is the chart of one of the most ethereal events in recent history. There was nothing like Woodstock, nor will there ever be again. It was a one of a kind event. People traveled from all over the United States to gather in a field that was offered for the occasion by the dairy farmer who owned it. People went there and then waited days for it to begin. What began as a profitable weekend concert, took on a life of its own, and after much work to make it happen, it was finally declared *free* just before opening day. There had been devised no way to keep people out, and nothing did keep people out except the massive traffic jams along the roads.

At 5:07 p.m. on Friday, August 15, 1969, Richie Havens stepped onto the stage, forced by a disorganized committee to start the proceedings . . . and the crowd cheered. It took a few minutes to sort out the microphones and wires before Richie said or sang one word. I've set the chart for 5:15 in the afternoon when Havens sang *Freedom*.

The event had a 0 Scorpio Midheaven, and a feeling realm of planets in the eighth house—Pluto, Moon, lunar nodes, and Mercury—which wholly describes the event. Capricorn was on the Ascendant, an odd sign to represent a crowd of hippies; but the ruler, Saturn, was in the fourth house of home. All those hippies made a temporary home right there in that field. Saturn was in Taurus and conjunction the Midheaven-Nadir axis axis.

What was the tension with Saturn? The biggest tension was being able to supply all these people with the comforts of home—

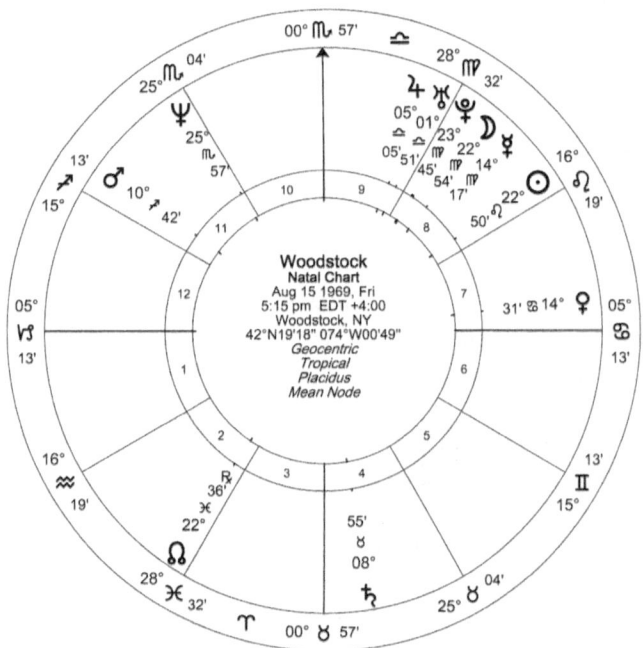

food, water, facilities, and medical attention—an enormous feat. Everyone who worked to serve the crowd during the event had volunteered. Everything had been considered. There was even a tent erected for people who might have a "bad trip."

Fortunately, there was only one death at the event: a volunteer worker who had fallen asleep in an adjacent field and was accidentally run over by a tractor. One could say that this worker was a hero because if there had been any lack of order, any lack of volunteer workers, a stampede of 50,000 people would have caused devastation of megalithic proportions.

In the Sabian dictionary, 0 Scorpio is "a crowded sightseeing bus on a city street." The symbol is about people gathering together to "view" the culture of their times, and that is what these people were doing there in 1969, viewing the last vestiges of the phenomena of the 1960s, the counter-revolution. It had just wound itself to a finish, and everyone present did not want it to disappear. We still don't want it to disappear. Of the 0 Scorpio degree, astrologer Dane Rudhyar says:

> Individuals come from a variety of places and backgrounds to "commune" in new awareness of a greater whole of human existence, an organized whole with its own rhythms of multifarious activities. The process of "initiation" into collective values is reaching the feeling nature. We are dealing with a group experience of a vast collective achievement."

He could have been talking about Woodstock. The words acknowledge both the achievements that had been made in the 1960s, and the initiation into new collective values. Dane says that it is reaching a feeling nature, and that is what everyone at Woodstock was experiencing. When Richie Havens passed away in 2013, he had his ashes spread over that field. When he performed there in 1969, he was experiencing his first Saturn return, at 8 Taurus. It was his personal coming of age event.

The chart of Woodstock is notable for the stellium in the eighth house. There was the usual experience that comes with rock concerts when everything is permeated with sexuality, but even more than that was the understanding that this was a deep and important collective experience. The 1960s had emphasized its revolution with the Uranus-Pluto conjunction in Virgo, when people were redefining health and well-being, incorporating ideas on getting "back to nature." The Virgo stellium at Woodstock celebrated nature, and with the Pisces end of the lunar node, also the need for mysticism and meditation and the alternative solution.

The Uranus-Jupiter conjunction in Libra, as a feeling realm, can carry fanaticism, such as the need for the replacement of capitalism (Uranus ruled the second house of commerce) with a version of some sort of under-the-table barter system or even free government support (Jupiter ruled the twelfth). This energy wants something and feels that it is entitled to it.

The most significant feeling realm in the chart is the Sun-Neptune square. As a function of standing up to be counted, the Sun feels muted and veiled, vague, but possibly very spiritual. If this were the chart of an individual, there would be work needed to incorporate the idealism and the artistry into the individuality. But it is a mass experience, a vision for everyone.

There is a museum in Bethel, New York, dedicated to the preservation of this iconic event in history. The field is still inhabited by cows. If you go there, be sure to wear some flowers in your hair, and feel the dream lingering in the air. (Chart Data Rating: AA)

The Twin Towers

If any location in America is imbued with emotional energy, it is the One World Trade Center in New York. Even before 9/11 there were ghosts in the buildings. One blogger named Jerry Spivey who worked there prior to and during 9/11 as a night maintenance person writes that he regularly saw benign spirits walking the building. On the morning of September 11 he received warning hints from these spirits that something unusual was going to happen that day, and since they lived in the spirit world, why wouldn't they know about it? When the first plane hit, Jerry immediately ordered his crew to evacuate, and then later got himself out just prior to both buildings crashing down.

It is not just ghosts who will populate a location even after the buildings themselves have been replaced. It is the emotional dimension that will remain until emotional work is done to clear the trauma from the area. Anyone who works in the new building is surrounded daily with that energy, even in a slightly different spot, and especially people who have matching zodiac degrees. It is important to make conscious decisions to pray or emit understanding for the souls who have left themselves behind there.

Mercury in the chart on the Ascendant is a standout feature,

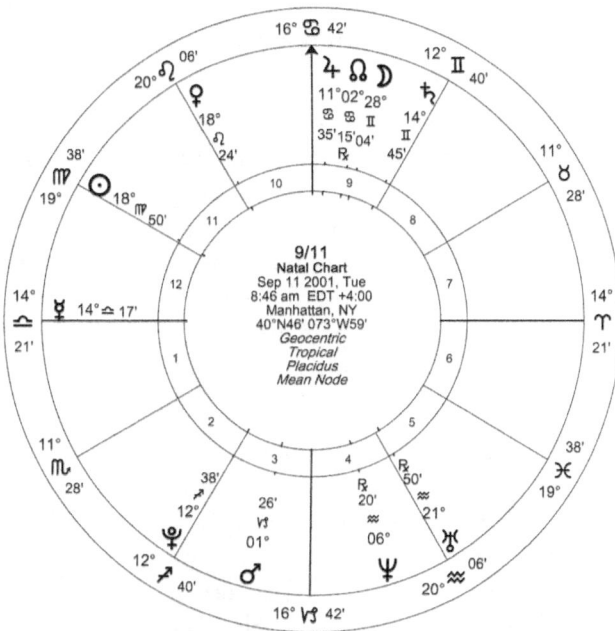

square Jupiter on the Midheaven. This is the core of the chart's heart and soul. If we look at the lunar nodes first to see what sort of trust profile is there, we see that Mars is with the lunar nodes in the third and ninth houses. Trust is present as long as there is communication about ideals and beliefs. Mars rules the seventh house of "the other," i.e., everybody. It is a picture of what can go wrong when ideologies become too forceful and too unique, without the accompanying ideology that we are in essence all the same.

The designers of the new One World Trade Center decided not to include a space for the Windows on the World lounge at the top of the building. Who could sip wine and converse in that location? While there are places to dine there, they are not recommended by many. The energy is all wrong for dining. There now is a whining noise from wind against the corners of the building, which can be heard for blocks around. It is said to be a design flaw. It didn't start whining until after hurricane Sandy hit the area, so maybe it is water. In any case, it sings two notes at once, and we could say, one for each of the lost towers.

There are two other feeling realms in the horoscope of 9/11 which should be mentioned, and they are both oppositions, which can easily be assigned to victims and perpetrators if that's how people want to see it. Venus in Leo is opposed to Uranus in Aquarius. Venus is the more personal planet and it rules the Ascendant in this case. The people in the building were hit quickly, and they needed to get out of the building quickly, but many of them were told to stay in place. The rigidity that can happen with fixed signs can interfere with Uranian creativity.

Meanwhile, Saturn was opposition Pluto at 12 Sagittarius on the cusp of the third house, putting great pressure on thoughts and words. It is also at the degree which is the Ascendant for the United States Sibley horoscope. Perhaps we have much to say about this country that has not yet been said. On September 11, most of us were just dumb-struck. News anchors bantered because that is what they do, but everyone felt the separation between self and self, and self and others. We wanted to cling to someone, as people fluttered down from the top of the towers, holding hands.

The Sun and the Moon in the chart are basically peregrine, although the Moon is near the lunar nodes. They are both in signs ruled by Mercury, again steering attention toward the main theme in the horoscope—what we think and believe, and what we say, can become so tantamount that we create separation.

If the new building is to resonate with the event that occurred and help it heal, it needs to be used for very ethical trade. Communication can be free of high-mindedness only when the trading of information and commodities is done in a fair manner. If you visit the building, don't eat there; the food is imbued with thoughts that stick in the craw. Say a prayer for the lingering souls.

Disneyland

It has been said by promoters that Disneyland is the happiest place on earth, and a place that inspires, a place to dream. If there are any sinister plots by the Illuminati to take over the world through the designs of Walt Disney, perhaps it will be seen in the horoscope of the opening day of the park. First, though, it was a little tricky to know which chart to choose because there was an opening day for exclusive guests, and an opening day for the general public, and it seems that Disneyland, well, Disneyland should be for everybody.

For the public the opening day was Sunday, July 17, 1955. Fifteen thousand guests had been invited, some as early as 2:30 p.m., although 5:30 p.m. was the official time, and around 13,000 people crashed the gates with counterfeit invitations. The park called it Black Sunday because there were so many things that went wrong, but since so many people came, well, it is suggestive of the nature of Disneyland, the feeling that it is somehow owned by the people, the way many of us think that McDonald's is "ours."

There is no perfect horoscope, not even for Disneyland. If an astrologer were asked to elect a chart for the grand opening—and probably this did not happen—it would be very difficult to choose a time. Where does Saturn go? Do you let it rule the concession stands and the money? If we use the most official time we have, that is *exactly* where Saturn is, ruling the money.

On Sunday the 17th, the press pass tickets were set for 5:30 p.m. The press allowed the entire United States to be present at Disneyland for ninety minutes while they filmed live inside the park. Neptune was in the tenth house, a good place for Neptune to be if the business is creating dreams. But what are all those planets doing in the eighth house?

Well, let's take a closer look. The time of 5:30 p.m. puts the lunar nodal axis not that far from the Ascendant-Descendant, appropriate for the performing aspect of Disneyland. The nodes are sextile and trine Neptune in the tenth house. That is appropriate for the feeling that there is trust as long as there can be a stage to "make dreams come true." Children are represented by Venus ruling the fifth house, and Venus is in Cancer. The children feel safe, at home. Venus is close to Mercury in the same sign, always the suggestion of idealization, and it rules the Descendant—those trustworthy and wonderful park operators! The Moon is there too, bringing comfort the old-fashioned way, from within the family.

So far, so good! The Ascendant is in Sagittarius for inspiration, and the Midheaven is in Libra, also ruled by Venus, and a lovely sign for making people feel as if they are at a party given just in their honor.

But Pluto is in the eighth house, and he is not Mickey's dog! It rules the eleventh house, which we could say is the profits from the business, and that is the house where Saturn resides, which takes care of the money. Neither Pluto nor Saturn are in any fourth harmonic relationships with anything; they simply are put to work without becoming part of any emotional dimension. The eighth house, though often the house of death, in this case is the house of collective investors; but there is some mystery there.

Jupiter and Mars are conjunct in Leo, and at first glance it looks like an abundance of fun, maybe too much; but it has been said that Mars in Leo can get away with murder, and indeed, if you have been on the Pirates of the Caribbean ride there is more than just murder to assault your ethical standards there. The messages are not "children friendly," but neither are traditional fairy tales, which we have traditionally read to children. We all want to be a little bit scared sometimes, and children will discover evil in the world soon enough anyway. Jupiter-Mars in the eighth house is the feeling that adventure can bring transformation, and also very real danger.

The Uranus-Sun conjunction in Cancer can suggest the ev-

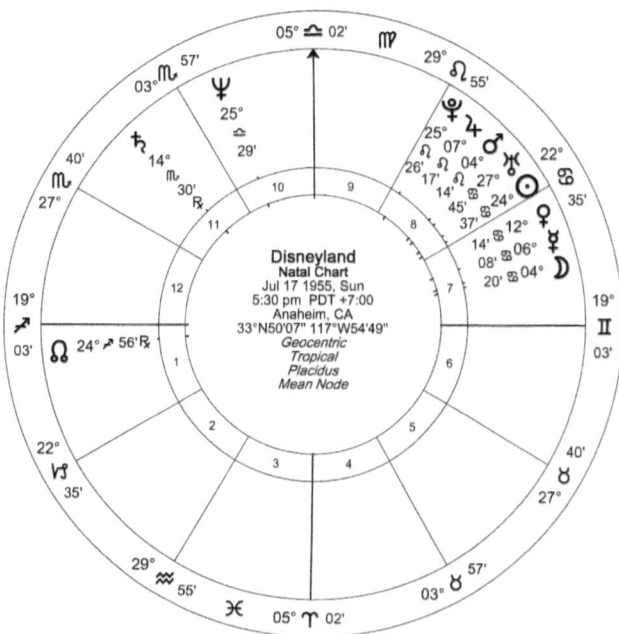

er-growing technology that Disney always uses. The Neptune square to the Sun describes the fantasy. All is illusion and tricks. Like Uranus, Neptune rules the third house. It has been said by the conspiracy theorists that messages have been planted in the Disney cartoons for a long time now—secret, subliminal messages. I have seen a few of them myself, although I think it is only the creators playing tricks on the producers. Who knows?

Things are not what they seem, and maybe they are more dangerous than we know. Like an old fashioned carnival, there can be a point at which everything seems to be nonsense, and we welcome it, as an escape from our everyday dull and tedious life. Many of us are only vaguely aware of that feeling, but it is the whole reason we go there—to have our world turned upside down and inside out.

If you go to Disneyland, never mind if anything in the chart matches your own chart; you are there to be taken for a ride.

Disneyland sits on the 33rd latitude, which is probably why the exclusive club at the park is called Club 33—unless you believe that Walt Disney was a Mason of the highest order, and then it might be for another reason altogether. If you are interested, the book by Walter Mosely, *Latitude 33—the Key to the Kingdom*, tells about the mystery of the carousel at the entrance to the park and why it was moved from its original position, which was on an important ley-line through the park. Mosely's belief is that it was moved because it was considered too dangerous (Uranus dangerous!), and it could pull people through a portal to another dimension . . . or something like that.

Places Just for You

I worked as a travel agent for many years, and became interested in helping people decide where they might want to go in this world. There are books published on astro-cartography, but if you understand anything about astrology, and you have an astrology program with the "maps" button, it is simple to see the points in the world where your natal planets fall on the angles, the Ascendant-Descendant axis, and the Midheaven-Nadir axis.

Those places in the world put great emphasis on the planets indicated, and bring them into focus for you. For instance, if you are a writer, and your Mercury is not on an angle, see what happens when you travel to the place where Mercury is on the Midheaven, or on any angle. Find out if you discover anything new about your writing. If you want to connect with your sensuality, go to where Venus is on an Ascendant or Descendant. It happened for me in Paris! Woohoo! What a perfect place for that to happen.

Because I did a lot of traveling myself, I experienced many of these things. I was born in California, but when I was born, the Sun was at high noon in New York City, and smack on the Midheaven there. Though it is not my horoscope, nor will I ever live there, when I traveled to New York City, I found that I held my head a bit higher in New York City than I did anywhere else. I felt empowered. I walked tall with big strides . . . and that was before I even thought about the astro-cartography.

When I went to Hawaii the first time, the place where the Sun was just coming up over the horizon in Kauai when I was born, I felt wonderfully warm and cheerful there. Yes, yes, I know . . . everybody feels that way in Hawaii; but I know a woman who felt horrible in Hawaii. She hated it there. Everything went wrong for her. It was discovered that in Hawaii, on the day she was born, Mars and Pluto had moved to angles in the horoscope. This means that in that location she faces greater challenges to her reputation and her self-expression.

Aside from astro-cartography, your own home can be imbued with past events that occurred there, and you may not be able to find out through normal resources what the events were. Before you purchase a house, it is best to ask questions; but if there is a heavy feeling in your house that you don't think you have created yourself, hire a professional, a house psychic. You have been drawn to that house for a reason, so look within. Do the work. Check your horoscope. The energy on our Earth is not separate from who we are. Ask the people who work in Washington D.C., or those who live at the Vatican. They know.

Conclusion

I hope that there have been some ideas or suggestions in this book that have helped some of you to move forward with the study and use of astrology in the way I've presented it. Astrology has meant so much in many lives. It has helped to identify the energies around a person, which are reflecting the energies within, and has given terminology to some of the phenomenon which would otherwise be upsetting. It might be crazy fun at Disneyland when Winnie the Pooh encounters his nightmare world, but we cannot live with a steady diet of nonsense. Astrology brings some order.

There are many things I would like to share here, but it is better presented in another book, if I ever get the time and the passion to do it, or if world events do not overtake my explanations of them. I believe that, for we humans, time is cyclical and spiral, as we repeat our themes on ever more widening gyres, as William Butler Yeats once said. If we are able to widen our travel, we ascend, and experience a version of life that is more expansive.

The important "building" aspects, the fourth harmonic, also have expanded versions of themselves. The widest one of which I'm aware is the alignment of the solstice tilts of our Earth in fourth harmonic position to the Galactic Center, which we are experiencing at this time. You can call it the Galactic Alignment. We return to fourth harmonic position with the galaxy center every 6.5 thousand years, but more dramatically every 13,000 years, at which point we are now.

These things have been spoken of by many. My favorite authors on the subject are Ken Carey who wrote *Starseed Transmissions* (1994), and Pierre Tielhard de Chardin, who wrote the *Phenomenon of Man* and *The Future of Man* almost a century ago, and who understood very well the nature of man's ability to transform. We transform through tension; there is no other way. We evolve during those fourth harmonic episodes in our life, whether it happens periodically during a lifetime or periodically in the life of mankind.

The spiraling force may appear to be supportively gradual, and while that might be truth, as humans we feel moments of tension. In 2020, Pluto and Saturn form a conjunction at the end of the year—in fact, on December 21, the day of the winter solstice! Yes, we've seen that conjunction before, but not during a fourth harmonic aspect of the earth tilt to the Galactic Center. Surely it heralds the new age of Aquarius (although it is some time coming yet), just as the Bethlehem star heralded the age of Pisces with a Saturn-Jupiter conjunction in Pisces. Why not?

I don't know what it all means in its entirety, but I know that it is important. I know that any emotional work we do at this time will prepare us for the next evolutionary leap of mankind which many great minds have been talking about. It takes no special talent to face our emotions; it only takes honesty, release of the ego, a handful of common sense, and a lot of compassion. It's a recipe. You can add your own spice, but if you don't do the work, you will slide right down that spiral, and have to do it all over again.

If you've read this book and wondered how to do this emotional work, you need a different book. This book is to point out where you can pinpoint your emotional work, and to begin to allow yourself to experience it. I personally like the book *Emotionally Healthy Spirituality (2013)* by Peter Scazzero, but it is a Christian-based book, so find another one if you have objections to the religious perspective.

Please appreciate and give honor to your own journey, no matter how difficult it has been so far. I don't believe our life is written in stone, though in childhood we depend so very much on the choices that our parents make. Know that your choices will always speak your horoscope, whether they are positive or negative ones. When your will aligns with the divine will, all will be well. When you have mastered a fourth harmonic aspect in your chart, it's because you are a brave soul.

Bibliography

De Beauvoir, Simone. *Memoirs of a dutiful daughter.* New York: Harper Publication, 1958.

Brady, Frank. *Endgame: Bobby Fischer's remarkable rise and fall—from America' prodigy the edge of madness to.* New York: Random House, 2011.

Butler, Susan. *East to the Dawn: the life of Amelia Earhart.* New York: De Capo Press, 2009.

Cayce, Edgar, and R. Smith. *The lost memoirs of Edgar Cayce—the life of a seer.* Virginia Beach, VA: ARE publications, 1997.

Christiansen, Clayton. *How will you measure your life?* New York: Harper's Business, 2012.

Dahmer, Lionel. *A father's story.* New York: William Morrow and Company, 1994.

Davenport, Guy. *Geography of the imagination.* Boston: David R. Godine publisher, North Point Press, 1981.

Erikson, Erik. *Identity and life cycle.* New York: W.W. Norton and Co., 1959.

Freud, Sigmund. *Civilization and its discontent.* First published in German,1930. English edition New York: W.W. Norton and Co., 1961

Freud, Sigmund. *Motivation and personality.* New York: Harper and Brothers, 1954.

Green, Jeffrey. *Pluto: evolutionary journey of the soul: volume I.* St. Paul, MN: Llewellyn, 1985.

Gottlieb, Robert. *Sarah: The life of Sarah Bernhardt.* New Haven, CT: Yale University press, 2010.

Hawking, Jane. *Traveling to infinity: the true story behind the theory of everything.* London: Alma Books movie tie-in, 2014.

Henner, Marilu and L. Henner. *Total memory makeover.* New York: Gallery Books, 2012.

Hilty, James. *Robert Kennedy, brother protector.* Philadelphia: Temple University Press, 2000.

Jung, Carl. *Man and his symbols.* New York: Doubleday, 1964.

Chart Ratings and Sources

Paulo Coelho, rated A, source: himself
Noel Ty, rated A, source: himself
Janis Joplin, rated AA, source: BC
Van Morrison, rated A, source: himself
Robert Kennedy, rated A, source: mother
Denzel Washington, rated AA, source: BC
David Blaine, time unavailable; speculation
Prince William, rated AA, source: BC
Claude Monet, time unavailable; speculation
Charles Manson, rated AA, source: BC
Martha Washington, rated B, source: family bible
Edgar Cayce, rated C, source: Doris Agee
Gordon Ramsay, rated AA, source: BC
Rosa Parks, rated C, source: anonymous
Terry Ryan, time unknown, speculation
Edward Snowden, rated AA, source: BC
Stephen King, rated A, source: himself
Steffi Graf, rated AA, source: BC
W. B. Yeats, rated AA, source: BC
Jean Paul Sartre, rated AA, source: BC
Barack Obama, rated AA, source: BC
Elizabeth Smart, time unknown, speculation
Florence Nightingale, rated DD, speculation
Jim Morrison, rated AA, source: BC
J. K. Rowling, time unavailable, speculative

Marilu Henner, time unavailable, speculative
Clayton Christiansen, time unavailable, speculative
Angelina Jolie, rated AA source: BC
Amelia Earhart, rated AA, source: BC
Sarah Bernhardt, rated B, source: A, Gold
Martin Litton, time unavailable, speculative
Jules Leotard, source: Astrotheme, rectified
Jeffrey Toobin, time unavailable, speculative
Mohanlal, time unavailable, speculative
Jeffrey Dahmer, rated AA, source: BC
Fred Rogers, rated A, source: himself
Edward Gorey, time unavailable, speculation
Stephen Hawking, rated X, rectified
Leo Buscaglia, rated A, source: himself
Bobby Fischer, rated B, source: F. Brady
Simone de Beauvoir, rated AA, source: BC
Jean Paul Sartre, rated AA, source: BC
Lauren Bacall, rated B, source: herself
Humphrey Bogart, time unavailable, speculative
Marie Curie, rated AA, source: BC
Pierre Curie, rated AA, source: BC
Pearl Harbor, rated AA, well documented
Woodstock, rated AA, well documented
911, rated AA, well documented
Disneyland, rated AA, source: ticket stubs

www.ingramcontent.com/pod-product-compliance
Lightning Source LLC
Chambersburg PA
CBHW020052170426
43199CB00009B/256